T0129223

FROM MOURNING

to

PRAISE

*A Biblical Guide
through Grief and Loss*

D O U G L A S   K N O X

WESTBOW
P R E S S®
A DIVISION OF THOMAS NELSON
& ZONDERVAN

This book is a work of non-fiction. Unless otherwise noted, the author and the publisher make no explicit guarantees as to the accuracy of the information contained in this book and in some cases, names of people and places have been altered to protect their privacy.

WestBow Press books may be ordered through booksellers or by contacting:

WestBow Press
A Division of Thomas Nelson & Zondervan
1663 Liberty Drive
Bloomington, IN 47403
www.westbowpress.com
1 (866) 928-1240

Because of the dynamic nature of the Internet, any web addresses or links contained in this book may have changed since publication and may no longer be valid. The views expressed in this work are solely those of the author and do not necessarily reflect the views of the publisher, and the publisher hereby disclaims any responsibility for them.

Any people depicted in stock imagery provided by Thinkstock are models, and such images are being used for illustrative purposes only. Certain stock imagery © Thinkstock.

ISBN: 978-1-5127-8896-9 (sc)
ISBN: 978-1-5127-8897-6 (hc)
ISBN: 978-1-5127-8895-2 (e)

Library of Congress Control Number: 2017908357

Print information available on the last page.

WestBow Press rev. date: 06/14/2017

CONTENTS

ACKNOWLEDGEMENTS

How does one express journey that begins in grief and ends with joy? No one completes it without help. Here are a few of the people who have helped me through my odyssey.

More than anyone else, my first wife Marie (1957-2003) showed me what selfless love looks like. She lived to help others, and set an example that my three daughters and I still follow.

During the dark days before and after Marie's death, my best friend, Art Chenevy, stood by me while I imploded. Other friends helped in ways they never knew. These include Jack and Sherma LeVeck, Bill Culler, Eric Abel, Matt Potosky, Kathy Ruffner, Bruce Wilkinson, and Diane Park. Thank you all.

Four of my seminary professors have been especially helpful in preparing me for the writing project. These are Daniel Hawk, my primary Old Testament instructor; Paul Overland, who instilled a love for the Hebrew language; Joanne Ford Watson, whose course on the theology of suffering was transformative; and Dawn Morton, who helped get the book started.

Special thanks go to my pastor and mentor, John Bouquet, who let me fly without a tether while I developed the curriculum that became the material for *From Mourning to Praise*.

Most of all, this book stands because of my wife Patty's help. Through multiple readings, and often rigorous editing, she caught typos and spellings errors, sharpened my prose, and helped me cut through the haze to make clearer copy. She has made the book what it is.

Finally, to the God who rescues those who grieve, I offer this as my praise to you.

I will perform my vows to you,
   that which my lips uttered
   and my mouth promised when I was in trouble....
Come and hear, all you who fear God,
   and I will tell what he has done for my soul.
I cried to him with my mouth,
   and high raise was on my tongue.

—Psalm 66:13b-14, 16-16

Doug Knox

INTRODUCTION

What to Expect from this Book

Go into any typical church on a Sunday morning, and you likely will find two occurrences. In public, people will tell you they are "Fine. Doing well. Couldn't be better." Greetings flip over the tongue like the file cards on a Rolodex. The singing time rings with choruses expressing gratitude, adoration, and praise for God. He is good. On the surface, joy is the order of the day. Everyone is glad to be in the Lord's house.

If we could see beneath the surface, however, a different story would begin to emerge among the individuals. Diana, who sits in the fifth row back on the left, lost her son twenty-three years ago in a Sunday morning auto accident. Her God has become distant. She has been unable to worship in a meaningful way since.

Matthew, one of the deacons, has moved to the back corner so he can leave the service early. Two weeks ago, his new warehouse manager, a kid half his age who touted a business degree and an attitude, hauled the entire work crew onto the warehouse floor so he could announce the names of the people who would lose their jobs to restructuring. Matthew was fifth on the list. He and his wife have never been rich, but he has been faithful as a breadwinner. Now, he wonders how he can find another job at his age in this economy.

Jennifer, a vibrant presence among the teens, receives almost weekly compliments on how "sold out" she is for Christ. Several young men in the youth group have asked her out, but her response is always the same. She needs to maintain focus. The truth is darker than what she reveals. She was molested by an uncle when she was ten years old and now finds it impossible to trust men. She hides her shame behind her smile.

These three suffer in silence because they have no other options. For them, God is not a God they can approach. They learned from the Bible that he dwells on the praises of his saints. Therefore, they need to praise. He is a God who forgives, so they must forgive. He refuses to hold grudges, so they should drop theirs.

Week after week, while the church lifts up praise, Diana, Matthew, and Jennifer do their best to stifle their grief and pretend that their worship has more substance than unflavored rice cakes. They are not bad people. They love the Lord. They just do not realize their grief is allowed to have a voice.

What to Expect from This Book

If you are like Diana, Matthew, or Jennifer, and wonder how—or whether— you can take your pain to God, I have good news. You can. The Bible shows us that God has walked your path, and he cares about you. He is also is eager to hear your complaint. If you suffer, this book is for you. However, I need to clarify what the book will and will not try to do. First, the things that the book will *not* attempt to do:

- *From Mourning to Praise* will not argue that God uses suffering to balance the good and evil in your life. It will not tell you that if you suffer, God must be punishing you for something you did in the past. That philosophy is only a form of Christian karma and a tool to manipulate through shame.
- This book will not promise miracle cures. It will not try to make your pain go away or manipulate your expectations with success stories about those who have achieved joy-filled lives after their losses. The Bible does not support this kind of mechanical expectation from God.
- Nor will this book call you to equate spirituality with happy feelings. It will not force you to pretend you are happy when you are not, and it will not cast blame on you while you mourn.

Those are the negatives. Here are some of the positive goals that the book will pursue:

- *From Mourning to Praise* will show you how to plead your case before God. It will teach you how to seek God's face in your dark hours and encourage you to cry out loud to God with your complaint.

- The book will call you to take your difficulties to God when all you have at your disposal is grief.
- The book will guide you in the art of encountering God during the most severe times in your life. Every biblical follower of God wrestled with these issues. You likewise have a right to approach God in your grief—out loud.

The Structure of the Book

This book will move through three major themes. Part 1 is introductory and necessarily philosophical. The section introduces the issue of theodicy, which deals with the problem of evil. If God is good, why does he allow suffering to exist in the world? Part 1 will examine three Western approaches to the question.

- At one extreme lies radical atheism, popularized by the late cosmologist, Dr. Carl Sagan and by evolutionary biologist Dr. Richard Dawkins. Under their view, God does not exist. Therefore, suffering has nothing to do with any "why" questions. It is part of the structure of the universe. It just is.
- In 1981, Rabbi Harold S. Kushner published his book, *When Bad Things Happen to Good People*. According to Kushner, a loving God exists who wishes happiness for good people, but he cannot control all events. Some suffering exists in spite of his wishes.
- Finally, we have the biblical view that declares a holy and all-powerful God who suffers alongside his creatures. God is the creator, sustainer, and redeemer of his creation, but he also participates *in* his creation. He uses the suffering in the world to bring about a greater end.

This section will defend the third position and argue that human beings are hardwired for meaning. Only a loving and all-powerful God can give us an ultimately satisfying answer to the questions that arise from our deepest pain. After introducing the three positions, this part of the book will examine God's purpose for suffering from the standpoint of the book of Job in the Bible. Job will form the foundation for the rest of the study on grief and loss.

Part 2 moves to several Psalms of lament. The book of Psalms in the Bible is a collection of songs and hymns directed to the LORD and written in poetic form. The psalms of lament call for deliverance during periods of profound suffering. If we catalog the Psalms, the largest single category consists of the individual cries of lament, in which a single person calls to the Lord for deliverance. The writers penned their grief poems because they knew God not only cared about the way they felt, but also was able to do something about it.

This section will explain lament in contemporary terms. It will encourage you to practice lament the way the people in the Bible practiced it. Most importantly, it will map the journey from lament to praise. All the Psalms fall between those two poles of lament and praise, and all show the petitioner's desire to return to praise. The Psalms build their theology by recounting what God has done for his people. This book's title, *From Mourning to Praise*, draws on that reality.

Part III moves to the New Testament to discuss the larger understanding of suffering that grew from the perspective of Jesus' life, death, and resurrection while he was on the earth. The New Testament writers, having witnessed these events, addressed the subject of suffering from the point of view of Jesus' completed work on the cross. Hope and joy, for example, become connected to eternity, because they are rooted to the certainty of Christ's promise to return and restore the creation to perfection. When the New Testament frames God's purpose in suffering from this global perspective, we start to understand our grief and losses as part of his eternal plan.

This understanding does not mean that our suffering becomes unimportant. The New Testament never minimizes our tears. It never tells us to put them away and get on with praise. It calls us to set our eyes on the eternal in the midst of the temporal and promises a future beyond our imagining.

Your Role as a Reader

From Mourning to Praise is a Christian book, but you do not need to be familiar with the Bible or even be a Christian to read it. You can be a skeptic.

Since suffering is universal, we all share the experience. I have tried to communicate some of my insights on the subject in terms that most readers will be able to understand. Occasionally I slip into "Christian-ese," but that is only because the Christian faith is dear to me. When this happens, I try to explain the concepts in simple terms. The last chapter describes the Christian faith in more detail for those who might be interested in knowing Jesus personally. Those who are interested are welcome to read this section.

My hope in writing this book has been to help you come to grips with the struggle that has the potential to grow into a deep relationship with God. The book will encourage you to ask the questions you did not think you were allowed to ask and help build a sense of hope you never thought possible. From that foundation, your walk with God can become deeper than you ever imagined. Show me a man or woman whose understanding runs true, whose empathy toward others rises quickly, and whose mercy toward those who struggle cannot keep quiet, and I will show you a person who has wrestled with God. That struggle grows into the character of praise.

PART 1

THE PROBLEM OF SUFFERING

CHAPTER 1

Why Does God Allow Suffering?

O Lord Jesus, how long, how long
Ere we shout the glad song,
Christ returneth! Hallelujah!
Hallelujah! Amen. Hallelujah! Amen.[1]

Introduction: The Problem of Evil

A few years ago a student at the university where I worked posted a theological challenge on his dormitory room door. It was called "The Problem of Evil." His case went like this:

A good God would want to prevent evil.
An all-powerful God would be able to prevent evil.
Yet there is much evil in the world.
Therefore, either God is not all-powerful, or he is not good.

The student's question deals with the issue of theodicy. How can evil coexist with a good and all-powerful God? According to the student's argument, the mere presence of evil in the world makes the presence of an all-powerful and good God impossible. The certainty of his conclusion indicated that the student thought he possessed an airtight logical argument to prove once and for all that God cannot exist.

The first premise in the argument attacks God's nature. If God were good, he would want to prevent evil in the world, but he obviously has not done so. At the least, it suggests that he might not be a good God.

The second premise allows for his goodness but attacks his authority.

If he were all-powerful, he presumably would have done something about all the evil in the world. Perhaps he lacks the power to do anything about it.

According to the argument, the mere presence of evil removes God from his throne. Since evil exists in the world, God must be either uncaring, morally impotent, or both. On the surface, the argument on the problem of evil is formidable, even from a Christian perspective. Why has God let evil run rampant in the world? Given the two alternatives—that he lacks either the basic goodness to care about corruption or power to do anything about it—we have some serious consequences to consider.

Do we just give in, or might we be able to suggest an alternative? When we approach the problem from a different angle, we discover that the issue is far from settled.

The Argument from Our Need for a Good God

No one can deny that evil is a fact of reality. According to the student's case, evil is also proof positive against the existence of a God who should eliminate evil if he were loving and powerful enough. The presence of evil in the world drives God out of the world.

Or does it? Yes, skeptics appeal to the evil in the world to challenge God's existence and benevolence. It is a favorite tactic. But what happens when evil becomes monstrous?

In reality, people seek God as greedily as a thirsty man looks for water. I call this the argument from need. By itself, this fact does not make an airtight argument for God's existence, but it does show a side to the issue of evil that the student's argument from cynicism does not.

Those who remember the 9/11 attacks on the World Trade Center, the Pentagon, and United Flight 93, for example, also remember the nation's reaction to them. For a few weeks afterward, the United States became both patriotic and religious. "God Bless America" signs appeared alongside U.S. flags across the country. Commenting on the nation's reaction to 9/11, Joseph Stowell writes,

> Despite the tenacious grip of postmodern secularism on our nation, America was now gasping for breath with a sudden need for God. We need[ed] a transcendent reality to help us in a secular society that was unable to comfort

or heal. We were free to speak God's name again. He was now welcome in the hearts of Americans and in halls of power.[2]

The 9/11 attacks plunged our nation into the greatest pain in a generation, and we instinctively sought God for comfort from the wound that tore into our souls.

A similar reaction occurred after the Sandy Hook Elementary School shooting took place in Connecticut in 2012, when twenty early elementary school students and six adults were shot and killed at the school. As a state, Connecticut is far more secular than religious. Yet every single family that buried a child asked for a religious service.[3]

Likewise, twenty-four hours after the 2013 Boston Marathon bombing, the #PrayforBoston meme on Twitter peaked at almost a quarter of a million posts.[4]

When evil on a significant scale invades our lives, no one jumps up to say, "Eureka! Another proof that God does not exist!" Instead, evil drives people to look for solace in God's presence. People who otherwise ignore God suddenly become aware of how much they need him. We almost universally seek some sense of God's presence when we grieve. I believe God created us to exhibit precisely this reaction.

Therefore, reality argues against the student's argument. Those who claim the nonexistence of God by evil's existence alone build their case more from cynicism than reason.

Hardwired for Worship

Why does the presence of evil heighten rather than diminish our need for God?

Because we are hardwired to seek purpose. The need to recognize something greater than ourselves is an element of our being. Claus Westermann writes,

> Exalting is a part of existence. It is so much a part of it, that when one has ceased to exalt God, something else must be exalted. Then God can be displaced by a man, an institution, an idea. Exalting remains a function of

existence. World history demonstrates this. Man *must* exalt something, and without such exalting there can apparently be no existence.[5]

When evil appears to be triumphant, our natural reaction is to look for a power greater than the evil. God has planted this longing in us. When great evil occurs, our need for his solace becomes as strong as a child's need for a parent's comfort during a thunderstorm. The comfort we seek from God is not just symbolic. It has substantive meaning. Our desire for God's presence during crises stands as a demonstration of his being and nature.

One Person's Case for a Lesser God

These facts begin to put the student's argument into perspective, but they still leave the question about God's power unanswered. What about the dual presence of good and evil? How can these conflicting forces coexist? More importantly, which one is more powerful?

If we observe the student's argument carefully, we see that it makes a declaration about which of the two forces he believes has the final say in the world. According to the argument, the only sure sign of God's ultimate goodness should be his ability to eliminate evil from the cosmos. If evil continues to exist in the face of a good God, then God cannot be all-powerful. Therefore, God must not be able to have the last word on how the cosmos operates.

The issue is not an exaggeration or oversimplification. In 1981, Rabbi Harold S. Kushner (b. 1935) published a short but influential book, *When Bad Things Happen to Good People*. Kushner's book is a meditation on the biblical book of Job (rhymes with *robe*), which addresses this very issue. Why does a good God allow innocent people to suffer unjustly?

In a way, the book of Job is a fairytale in reverse. Job is an upright man whom God has blessed. God has given him and his wife great possessions, and they had with ten children. But as soon as we learn this about Job and his blessed life, everything is taken from him. He loses his fortunes to unwarranted attacks and freak accidents. His ten children die when a windstorm collapses the house around them. And Job himself falls prey to leprosy, a severe skin and nerve disease.

Worse, three of his friends arrive with every intention to offer him comfort, only to engage in an attack on his character because they are confident he has sinned. Meanwhile, all Job sees is the abrupt and total disappearance of the world he once knew. He pleads with a silent God. Kushner addresses the thematic difficulty in the book of Job this way:

> To try and understand the book and its answer, let us take note of three statements which everyone in the book, and most of the readers, would like to be able to believe:
>
> A. God is all-powerful and causes everything that happens in the world. Nothing happens without His willing it.
> B. God is just and fair, and stands for people getting what they deserve, so that the good prosper and the wicked are punished.
> C. Job is a good person.[6]

As Kushner affirms, virtually all believers in God assume these three premises. They define fairness. And, as he affirms, we cannot hold all three consistently. We remain comfortable as long as we stay within the first two—A.), God ordains everything, and B.), he is just and fair at the same time. That requires us to stay inside our little house, with the doors locked and the shutters drawn because we cannot face Point C.). Job is a good person, but he still suffers. When good people suffer, we discover the inevitable truth about the three premises. They all cannot stand together logically. We run into the adage, "When an irresistible force meets the immovable object, something has to give."

What gives? Does the irresistible force become resistible, or does the immovable object give way? After a lengthy consideration in his book, Kushner makes a difficult choice.

> Let me suggest that the author of the Book of Job takes the position which neither Job nor his friends take. He believes in God's goodness and in Job's goodness, and is prepared to give up his belief in proposition (A): that God is all-powerful. Bad things do happen to good people in this world, but it is not God who wills it. God would like

5

> people to get what they deserve in this life, but He cannot
> always arrange it. Forced to choose between a good God
> who is not totally powerful, or a powerful God who is not
> fully good, the author of Job chooses to believe in God's
> goodness....God wants the righteous to live peaceful,
> happy lives, but sometimes even He can't bring that about.
> It is too difficult even for God to keep cruelty or chaos
> from claiming their innocent victims.[7]

Rabbi Kushner's conclusion is anything but hasty. He committed to it after years of struggle with the issues. If you read the entire book, you will sense his deep sympathy for those who suffer. The fact that he published the twentieth-anniversary edition of the book stands as a testament to the book's popularity.

I say this out of respect for the man and his reasoning. I do not wish to attack Rabbi Kushner personally. Even so, I have to disagree with his conclusion about the way the author of Job perceives God's concession to the power of evil. As I did with the student's argument against God's goodness, I will take an indirect approach to the question regarding God's power.

The Argument from Our Hunger for Justice

Rabbi Kushner does not ask *whether* God exists. At this point, I stand with him. I believe God's being is undeniable. For Kushner, the issue involves God's relationship to evil. Is God powerful enough to circumvent evil, or has evil prevented him from carrying out many of the good things he has intended?

As we will see later, the Bible teaches that God is powerful as well as good—so powerful in fact that he ultimately will judge all evil. In the meantime, I would like to present one more observation on human longing in the face of severe injustice. I call it, "The argument from our hunger for justice," because of its similarity to the argument from need. Where the argument from need observes our need for a *caring* God, the argument for our hunger for justice demonstrates our need for a *just* God. Like the argument from need, it is more of an observation on our reaction to evil than an objective proof for God's existence.

We have argued for the human need to experience comfort and justice from a caring and just God, but we have left the original question unanswered. How does God deal with all the evil in the world?

The complete answer will come from the grand redemptive story in the Bible, for which Job plays a significant role. There we will witness three thematic arcs which will guide us through the course of this study.

The first is obvious enough. Natural evil, moral evil, suffering, longing, tears, and anguish are real, and the biblical characters do not hesitate to address them.

The second is less obvious than the first. Hope rises to the surface in the presence of loss, because the people who know God also know he is big enough to handle them with authority. In the briefest terms, hope is the conviction that God will turn the wrongs into right. It is the source of joy when we otherwise would be consumed by grief. Hope gives us a reason to continue when life otherwise would overwhelm us.

In the third arc, the Bible shows how God will bring justice to the world. He allowed suffering to enter the cosmos for a reason. He suffers and experiences injustice along with us. Ultimately God's personal suffering will become the unanticipated means by which he rescues the people he loves. Throughout the Bible, he shares human suffering, both to understand our pain and to rescue us from injustice.

Journal Entry

Each chapter will close with a journal entry. The goal of the book is to help you move from mourning to praise, but that movement is something you must commit yourself to doing. The journal entries are designed to assist you in your journey.

When medical specialists search for a cure for a disease, they begin by studying the disease itself. The more deeply they understand how the disease acts, grows, and reacts to stimuli, the better they will be able to find a means to stop it.

The same applies for our feelings. As painful as the process is, we need to be able to identify our pain as specifically as possible.

- At whom are you angry?
- What are your feelings toward God right now?

- What would you like to tell God?
- How would you like to feel toward God?

_____

_____

_____

_____

_____

_____

_____

CHAPTER 2

Job and the Problem of Suffering, Part 1: Moralistic Religious Solutions to the Problem of Evil

For I know that my Redeemer lives,
and at the last he will stand upon the earth.
—Job 19:25[8]

Introduction

I first encountered the book of Job during an Old Testament survey class when I was in my early twenties. My initial exposure to the book was less than stellar. After a compelling opening in the first two chapters, the book launched into a lengthy poetic discourse, in which Job and his three friends argued about who was right and who was wrong concerning God and his relationship to his people. The arguments seemed to go on forever.

Ironically, a few months later, a close Christian friend and I came to blows over the meaning of praise and its relationship to the Christian life. My friend had become convinced that the goal of the Christian life was to be ever positive, ever confident, ever smiling. When I questioned his praise-the-Lord-all-the-time mentality, our disagreement exploded. I realized our conflict lay with the same issue that challenged Job and his friends. We disagreed over the fundamental nature of God's relationship with his people.

I went back to the book, this time putting myself in Job's place. Job's questions concerning justice, praise, and joy became my issues, and the message clicked. The book became one of my favorites and has remained so ever since.

Worship in Job

The book of Job touches on any number of themes, but worship lies at its center. How do we relate to God, and how does God relate to us? Is worship a matter of pressing the right buttons, so that God will make us happy, or does it reflect a relationship that transcends circumstances? These fundamental questions lead to more nuanced issues in the theodicy question:

- Just how great is God?
- Can God handle the evil in the world?
- Does God care about his subjects when they suffer?
- Is God powerful enough to do anything about injustice?
- Is God really in control if he continues to allow all the evil to have free rein in the world?

Job presents a drama of evil at work in God's creation. For this reason, we begin our journey from mourning to praise by observing one of the men who struggled most deeply in his search for the truth about the God he worshiped. This chapter will look at the opening of Job to see what kind of light the book can shed on our questions.

God, Satan, and Job in the Cosmic Conflict (Job 1-2)

Job was a unique man. The Bible describes as "blameless and upright, one who feared God and turned away from evil" (Job 1:1). No other character in Scripture receives this accolade. He had seven sons and three daughters and owned eleven thousand animals that included sheep, camels, donkeys, and oxen.

Job's house was filled with worship. After the celebratory times, "Job would send and consecrate them, and he would rise early in the morning and offer burnt offerings according to the number of them all. For Job said, 'It may be that my children have sinned and cursed God in their hearts.' Thus Job did continually" (Job 1:5). Job was a man who loved God and was blessed by God.

But his blessed life was not to last for long. Immediately after the introduction, the narrator pulls back the curtain to reveal a troubling scene brewing in heaven:

Now there was a day when the sons of God came to present themselves before the LORD, and Satan also came among them. The LORD said to Satan, "From where have you come?" Satan answered the LORD and said, "From going to and fro on the earth and from walking up and down on it." And the LORD said to Satan, "Have you considered my servant Job, that there is none like him on the earth, a blameless and upright man, who fears God and turns away from evil?" Then Satan answered the LORD and said, "Does Job fear God for no reason? Have you not put a hedge around him and his house and all that he has, on every side? You have blessed the work of his hands, and his possessions have increased in the land. But stretch out your hand and touch all that he has, and he will curse you to your face."

—Job 1:6-11

The picture calls for close examination. In the opening, the sons of God appear before the LORD. The term likely means angels. When Satan appears among them, uninvited, God shows no surprise. In fact, he draws attention to the leading human player in the drama when he asks Satan, "Have you considered my servant Job...?" (Job 1:8).

God's term, "my servant Job," is a title that recognizes Job as one who stands in a favored position in God's hierarchy, one whom he knows personally. Where God affirms Job as a righteous man who is full of integrity, however, Satan sees him as an easy target. In Satan's opinion, Job has grown soft in his allegiance to God. God's very blessings have made him weak. Job loves God only because God has given him a prosperous life, and Satan is certain he can prove his case by doing nothing more than calling God to "touch all that he has."

The Question of Evil Personified

God and Satan are engaged in a cosmic chess match with each other, and Satan wants to turn Job into his sacrificial pawn. Job, meanwhile, is unaware that anything outside his visible world is taking place. More is involved with this challenge than just the loyalty issue. First, Satan is confident that God is less than good. In his mind, God has bought Job's allegiance by sham. Second, he is equally convinced that God is fallible. All Satan has to do is break Job's loyalty, and he will expose God's shell game.

His challenge takes us back to the question of evil, but with a twist. Now, evil has a face. Therefore, the question is no longer, "If God is all-powerful, should he not be able to prevent evil?" It becomes, "If God really cares, should he not want to stop the Accuser from hurting Job?"

Even God's integrity comes into question. Satan presents the challenge in such a way that it directs the blame toward God.

Interestingly, the LORD throws Satan's words back at him. In response to the accuser's understated, "touch all that he has," God answers, "Behold, *all that he has* is in your hand. Only against him do not stretch out your hand" (Job 1:12, emphasis added). God gives Satan virtual *carte blanche* over Job's circumstances. He can do whatever he wishes to Job's possessions, as long as he does not harm Job directly.

Of course Satan's term, "touch," is a euphemism. When Satan leaves the LORD's presence, four back-to-back events topple Job's world.

- The Sabeans attack the oxen and camels, killing all but one of the servants, who comes back to tell Job the devastating news (Job 1:14-15).
- The fire of God falls from heaven and burns up the sheep and shepherds. Again, only one servant lives to tell Job (Job 1:16).
- The Chaldeans raid the camels, killing all the servants in the process. Only one remains (Job 1:17-18).
- A wilderness wind strikes the house where Job's ten children feast, and kills them all. Only the servant lives (Job 1:19).

Earlier we introduced Rabbi Kushner's thoughts on the book of Job. He concludes that the problem of evil is too great for God. He writes, "God wants the righteous to live peaceful, happy lives, but sometimes even He can't bring that about. It is too difficult even for God to keep cruelty or chaos from claiming their innocent victims."[9]

Here in the book of Job, the LORD does not appear to be bothered by the prospect. In fact, he is the one who broaches the subject with Satan. The text suggests that God entices Satan, rather than the reverse.

It begins to shed light on one of the questions regarding the problem of evil. Even in this short peeling back of eternity, the writer shows that God is powerful. He never says, "Oops." This is a good thing because if we are going to have a satisfactory answer to the problem of evil, the answer must involve an all-powerful God.

At the same time, the text leaves the question of God's goodness unanswered. Why has he has allowed Satan to attack Job so brutally? Why does he refuse to retaliate? To answer these issues, we will need to dig deeper into the book.

Job's Reaction to Crisis

When Job hears the news that his fortunes are gone and his children are dead, his reaction is remarkable.

> Then Job arose and tore his robe and shaved his head and fell to the ground and worshiped. And he said, "Naked I came from my mother's womb, and naked shall I return. The LORD gave, and the LORD has taken away; blessed be the name of the LORD."
>
> In all this Job did not sin or charge God with wrong.
>
> —Job 1:20-21

Only a man of character would be able to make this kind of statement. Rather than cursing, Job worships.

When we approach Job's prayer, we need to be careful to remind ourselves about the literary form in the first two chapters. This section constitutes a narrative, a summary of events written in to emphasize a theme, and Job's prayer is only a small part of a much larger theme in the book. The underlying motif in the text is Satan's failure in a moral battle that he was sure he would win.

Therefore, as commendable as Job's reaction is, the Bible has no intention to universalize his statement of grief. It never tells us, "Go and do likewise." To the contrary, the conflict is far from over. Satan is about to return for a second round, and Job will stumble under the onslaught.

If we keep the larger picture in mind, however, we still can make at least two objective observations on Job's worship. First, his reaction takes place in the midst of shock. His short speech depicts a man who has yet to bear the weight of the questions to come during the long course of his grief. To Job's credit, it shows the discipline that he has come to know in his life. He trusts his God in every circumstance, whether it is good or bad. But this expression of faith still takes place early, before the deep pain sets in.

Second, and perhaps more importantly, we need to recognize that Job's reaction is not spontaneous. In its rush to avoid grief, modern Western culture has lost sight of physical expressions of grief. In contrast, notice the sequence of Job's deliberate acts:

- He arose.
- He tore his robe.
- He shaved his head.
- He fell on the ground.
- He worshiped.

When biblical narratives list a series of actions in short succession, as the text does here, they become significant. Here his acts are non-verbal affirmations of grief, indicating that a person's world has spun out of control.

Our typical reaction to sudden tragic news borders on denial. Our actions betray an attempt to maintain control. We sit down. We compose ourselves. Then we start to plan. We make telephone calls. We need to connect. We have to prepare. We have to *do* something. This quote from a recent *Christianity Today* article illustrates the point.

> We live in a culture that tries to avoid grief. We've discarded many of the cultural indicators of mourning: Widows don't wear black for a year; mothers who lose their children no longer cut their hair; we've given up on sackcloth and ashes....Christians have participated in this denial. Mortality and grief are rarely mentioned from the pulpit. Many churches have moved their graveyards from the center of town to the suburbs so we don't have to be reminded of death as we walk into the sanctuary on Sunday mornings.[10]

Western culture, including the Christian culture, has come to a place where grief is more of a problem to be eliminated than a part of life to be affirmed. In his words and actions, Job speaks the language of lament.

A lament is an act of worship that rises out of grief. Part 2 of this book will develop this concept in detail. For now, let me list three reasons why lament is acceptable worship. First, it calls to the Lord out of weakness. It is not an attempt to look strong. It is the act of presenting ourselves in our brokenness to call on God to heal us.

Second, lament allows the worshiper to acknowledge his or her sorrow before the Lord. Lament never says, "Just praise the Lord anyway." Denying ourselves the privilege to grieve does not make the pain go away. In fact, denial only makes the pain worse. The Bible never tells us to pretend the pain is not there.

Third, lament affirms our trust in God to bring our grief to an end. Lament is a prayer of petition, or asking God to rescue us from a specific difficulty.[11] The only reason we do not see petition in Job 1:20-21 is because Job is still in shock. His moral case—to be able to have an audience before the LORD—will become very vocal later in the book.

A second Onslaught

In Job 2, Satan appears before the LORD a second time, only to be taunted. The LORD says,

> "Have you considered my servant Job, that there is none like him on the earth, a blameless and upright man, who fears God and turns away from evil? He still holds fast his integrity, although you incited me against him to destroy him without reason."

—Job 2:3

Satan remains unconvinced. He challenges the LORD to allow him to strike Job himself.

Again, the LORD gives Satan what he wants. He grants him permission to do anything short of killing Job. Satan strikes him with skin disease, probably leprosy. The text reads,

15

> So Satan went out from the presence of the LORD and struck Job with loathsome sores from the sole of his foot to the crown of his head. And [Job] took a piece of broken pottery with which to scrape himself while he sat in the ashes.
>
> —Job 2:7-8

The seeping sores signify a border breach in the body that was particularly hideous to the ancient Hebrews.

> The rotting appearance of the skin associated with a variety of disorders lumped together under the heading of "leprosy" is another potent source of uncleanness. This condition is closely connected with death...and the focus for its diagnosis is the erosion of the surface and the loss of integrity to the body's outer boundary.[12]

Without exception, the Bible equates leprosy with separation from God. Theologically, this only makes sense. God is altogether pure, and cannot be approached by anything unclean or impure. Under the Old Testament purity codes, people whose bodily integrity was compromised were unable to approach God through established worship. The compromise was physical, and therefore in a strictly technical sense, ceremonial. In the world of energized moral reasoning, however, such a compromise was only a step away from moral judgment and character assassination.

Job's Friends: Insufficient Understanding of God

In the body of the book, Job's three friends enter to offer their answer to the question regarding God's silence. The book identifies them as Eliphaz the Temanite, Bildad the Shuhite, and Zophar the Naamathite. The fact that these are three men from three different tribal groups shows the level of respect Job has earned. His suffering has caused an incredible stir. When his friends see him, they weep, tear their robes, and throw dust on their heads. Then, they sit on the ground for a week without saying a word (Job 2:12-13).

The week they spend in mourning is commendable, but the tree men are ultimately moralizers. They become champions of the moralistic religious point of view. The three are convinced that bad things do not happen to good people, and since bad things are happening to Job, he cannot be good. Eliphaz, Bildad, and Zophar's top-down efforts to fix Job produce only chaos.

Eliphaz, the Voice of Experience

Each man takes a shot at Job in turn. Eliphaz, who becomes the representative for the group, takes the lead. For this man, the truth is sure as tomorrow's sunrise. In fact, he is so certain of this that he can ask rhetorically,

> "Remember: who that was innocent ever perished?
> Or where were the upright cut off?"

> —Job 4:7

Eliphaz works from the vantage point of his observations.

> "*As I have seen*, those who plow iniquity and sow trouble reap the same."

> —Job 4:8, emphasis added

As he has seen. Is that not a comforting thought? Eliphaz, the panel of one, has determined this universal truth by his personal observations. Everyone who makes trouble has trouble come back to bite him in the end.

Compare the observation with his earlier rhetorical question, "Remember: who that was innocent ever perished?" For Eliphaz, the answer is so obvious that it requires no further thought. But let us pose the question as a factual one. In the Bible, who has perished, being innocent? Whenever I teach Job and ask this question, the audience usually pauses for a few seconds. The first two examples break the ice.

- Jesus, who died on the cross (Mark 15:37)
- Abel, the first man in history to die (Gen. 4:8; cf. Heb. 11:4)

Then, when the members begin to think through biblical history, the answers begin to fall like raindrops on a tin roof:

- The prophets (Matthew 23:31; Acts 7:52)
- The list of martyrs from Hebrews 11:36-38
- John the Baptist (Mark 6:14-29)
- Stephen the martyr (Acts 7:54-60)
- James the Apostle (Acts 12:2)
- A multitude of saints in church history

Eliphaz is wrong. Bad things, in fact, do happen to good people, and we too are mistaken if we try to deny the fact.

Unfortunately, Eliphaz's ignorance of the facts drives him on. To leverage his case against Job, he recounts a nightmare. The retelling makes Eliphaz the star of his show.

> Now a word was brought to me *stealthily*;
>> my ear received a *whisper* of it.
> Amid *thoughts and visions of the night*,
>> when deep sleep falls upon men,
>> dread came upon me and trembling,
>> which made all my bones shake.
> A spirit glided past my face:
>> the hair of my flesh stood up.
> It stood still,
>> but I could not discern its appearance.
>
> —Job 4:12-16a, emphasis added

Stealth. Whispers. Thoughts and visions of the night. Eliphaz has crafted these words to terrify. His nightmare emerges from one of the most elemental experiences in human fear, the unreachable and uncontrollable realm of the dead. A spirit has entered his presence and stands before him, plunging him into terror.

The scene is persuasive, and it is that very persuasiveness that calls us to be careful in our reaction to it. Yes, Eliphaz had a vision in the night, and yes, it was terrifying. But look at the situation from an unemotional standpoint. How does the mere presence of a poltergeist make a prophetic word more certain?

It does not. When we read the text carefully, we realize the nightmare is there for effect and nothing else. Still, Eliphaz is sure he has seen a vision from God.

Once he introduces the scene, Eliphaz's dream shifts from emotion to theology. While the spirit hovers before him, a voice utters,

> "Can mortal man be in the right before God?
>   Can a man be pure before his Maker?
> Even in his servants he puts no trust,
>   and his angels he charges with error;
> how much more those who dwell in houses of clay,
>   whose foundation is in the dust,
>   who are crushed like the moth."

—Job 4:17-19

The theological pronouncement from the disembodied voice becomes even more suspect than the nightmare. It begins with the conclusion, stated in the rhetorical form. "Can mortal man be in the right before God? / Can a man be pure before his Maker?" (Job 4:17).

If we take Eliphaz at his word, the answer is an unequivocal "No." The reason comes out of the structure of the cosmos. Eliphaz's moral universe, which he describes in the ghost's pronouncement, consists of three distinct levels:

- God's dwelling occupies the top tier, which is infinite, holy, altogether pure, unchangeable, and good. God is uncorrupted by sin.
- The realm of the angels lies below. It is spiritual by nature and immortal, lower than God but higher than humankind. In spite of angels' immortality, they are susceptible to error and therefore less trustworthy than God (Job 4:18).
- The human level is physical and mortal, altogether different from either the angels or God. Eliphaz describes humans as "those who dwell in houses of clay, / whose foundation is in the dust, / who are crushed like the moth." The human level lies far beneath the

realm of the angels. It is finite, unholy, impure, fickle, and flawed. Therefore, it must be even more distant from God.

Eliphaz's theological point is this: Before God, even his angels prove to be untrustworthy. Therefore, "those who dwell in houses of clay" inherit a significantly inferior position before God. The implication: Job, you are doomed before you even start. Do not try to defend your integrity, human. You have none.

Eliphaz presents a case for *absolute transcendence*. Transcendence means separation by a degree of greatness and is one of the foundational doctrines of the Bible. In Eliphaz's mind, everything rides on this doctrine. His fundamental assumption is that God and humanity are forever separate. God is so good, and his people are so flawed, that God could not trust anyone in his creation to do the right thing.

Eliphaz fails to see the trap in his argument. If this moral gap were unbridgeable, then he would be as untrustworthy as everyone else in the world. Where does Eliphaz come up with the notion that he, equally bound to a house of clay, can receive communication from the LORD, by a nightmare or otherwise?

The point where we must disagree with Eliphaz is the adjective, *absolute*. If God were absolutely transcendent, he would be separated completely from his creation. He would be so distant from human beings that he would be unable to communicate with anyone at all. God would be unknowable.

In spite of the logical flaw, Eliphaz remains confident in his thinking. Easy difficulties invite simple solutions, and for him the answer to Job's suffering is as simple as the theology that explains it.

> "As for me, I would seek God,
> and to God would I commit my cause....
> Behold, blessed is the one whom God reproves;
> therefore despise not the discipline of the Almighty."
>
> —Job 5:6, 17

What is Job supposed to do—fall and weep because someone finally has shown him the obvious?

Apparently, he is, because Eliphaz ends his speech with the words,

"Behold, this we have searched out; it is true. / Hear, and know for your good" (Job 5:27).

But to Eliphaz's horror, the unthinkable happens. Job rejects his buttoned-up theology and dares to speak for himself. Upon hearing him, Job's other two friends, Bildad and Zophar, bear their fangs. They parrot Eliphaz's theology while embellishing it with their approach. We will discuss their viewpoints only briefly.

Bildad, the Voice of Tradition

Bildad enters next. Where Eliphaz speaks from experience, Bildad resorts to tradition.

> "For inquire, please, *of bygone ages,*
> and consider *what the fathers have searched out.*"
>
> —Job 8:8, emphasis added

As to what the fathers have searched out, Bildad offers these comforting words:

> "Does God pervert justice?
> Or does the Almighty pervert the right?
> If your children have sinned against him,
> he has delivered them into the hand of their
>   transgression."
>
> —Job 8:3-4

Like Eliphaz, Bildad lives in a perfect moralistic universe. When people sin, God punishes them. All the old sages have said as much. Therefore, Job's children received what they deserved. All ten are dead because all ten must have sinned. These words constitute cruelty that borders on fanaticism.

Zophar, the Proverb Collector

Zophar's first speech takes place in Job 11, and he marks himself as a man who collects sayings. He argues that the Almighty's ways are higher than Job's (Job 11:7-10), and God knows a fool when he sees one (Job 11:11). Zophar demonstrates his complete disbelief of Job's integrity from the beginning.

> "Should a multitude of words go unanswered,
>   and a man full of talk be judged right?
> Should your babble silence men,
>   and when you mock, shall no one shame you?
> For you say, 'My doctrine is pure,
>   and I am clean in God's eyes.'
> But oh, that God would speak
>   and open his lips to you,
> and that he would tell you the secrets of wisdom.
>   For he is manifold in understanding.
> Know then that God exacts of you less than your guilt
>   deserves."

—Job 11:2-6

Job's Friends' Conclusion

Job and his friends enter into three cycles of debates (chapters 4-31), and their horns remain locked. By the end of the book, Job's friends' anger becomes almost explosive. Near the end, Eliphaz hurls this against Job:

> "Is not your evil abundant?
>   There is no end to your iniquities.
> For you have exacted pledges of your brothers for nothing,
>   and stripped the naked of their clothing.
> You have given no water to the weary to drink,
>   and you have withheld bread from the hungry.
> The man with power possessed the land,
>   and the favored man lived in it.

You have sent widows away empty
   and the arms of the fatherless were crushed."

                                                        —Job 22:5-9

The references to exacting pledges, securing the clothing from those who were devastated by the violation, withholding bread from the hungry, and sending the widows away empty-handed are not accidental. Exodus 22:21-24 and Deuteronomy 10:17-19; 14:27-29; 24:17-22 and 27:49 define social justice in these terms. These actions mark the boundary between blessing and cursing under the law covenant. Eliphaz's curse declares Job to be a fraud.

Job's Friends' Inadequate Understanding of God

Job's friends face a difficulty that plagues us to this day, and that is an oversimplified understanding of God and his creation. To state the issue metaphorically, they have tried to put God in a box and then tie the box up in a bow. Christian thinking that assumes a one-to-one correspondence between suffering and sin begins to think exclusively in horizontal terms. Thinking like this tries to reduce the world to two classes of people: the blessed (who are always right and always speak for God) and the cursed (who oppose God and are always wrong). A Christian caste society emerges, defined by those who are "in" as opposed to those who are "out."

Job's Inadequate Understanding of Justice

Job displays a deeper theological understanding of God than his friends, but ultimately he shares their moralistic reasoning. Job begins to shift from self-defense to self-justifying theology under the same moralistic cause-and-effect understanding of righteousness that his friends believe. In doing so, he crosses the line and begins to make unjustified demands on God. When we read Job's speeches, therefore, we need to watch out for error, but also remember his integrity against the backdrop of his suffering. As we examine the drama from our armchairs, we need to recognize the stress that grows out of excruciating pain. Our thinking and our vocabulary become self-centered and angry. The one in pain will not be able to reason like one who suffers nothing. Our study will recognize Job's error, but also take his situation into account.

Over the course of his suffering, he begins to direct his speeches away from his friends and toward his God. In the end, Job concludes that God is unjust. He tells his friends,

> "If indeed you magnify yourselves against me
>   and make my disgrace an argument against me,
> know then that God has put me in the wrong
>   and closed his net about me."

> —Job 19:5-6

Additionally, Job believes he can defend his righteousness before God:

> "As God lives, who has taken away my right,
>   and the Almighty, who has made my soul bitter....
> I hold fast my righteousness and will not let it go;
>   my heart does not reproach me for any of my days."

> —Job 27:2, 6.

Job has fallen prey to the same error that his friends hold, and that involves the assumption of a morally simple universe. He merely looks at the situation from the other side. We see his view in his words, "I hold fast my righteousness and will not let it go; / my heart does not reproach me for any of my days." He defines justice by its relation to himself rather than as an outworking of God's character. Job has maintained his integrity, yet he still suffers. Therefore, God has ignored Job's goodness. Walton and Longman explain,

> Job is not claiming that he is perfect; he only wants to be
> declared innocent of the sort of offenses that would have
> caused his dramatic downfall. He wants to face his judge,
> hear the charges and be given an explanation or—in the
> absence of such an explanation—be acquitted.[13]

When we place ourselves at the center of our moral universe, we lose our capacity to enjoy God. The same goes for Job. He can be satisfied only when he perceives God working on his behalf. Rather than regarding justice as God's perfect will carried out "on earth as it is in heaven," a self-centered view redefines justice by what satisfies him as an individual. In the extreme, this becomes narcissism. C.S. Lewis writes, "The problem of reconciling human suffering with the existence of a God who loves, is only insoluble so long as we attach a trivial meaning to the word 'love', and look on things as if man were the centre of them."[14]

Elihu, a More Benign Moralism

By the third round of arguments, Job and his friends enter a stalemate. At this point, a younger man named Elihu comes. Because of his youth, he has kept silent, but after the screaming match, he can contain himself no longer. According to the text, he "burned with anger at Job because he justified himself rather than God. He burned with anger also at Job's three friends, because they had found no answer, although they had declared Job to be in the wrong" (Job 32:2-3). Elihu is a breath of fresh air for several reasons:

- He respects those who are older and more experienced (Job 32:6).
- He listens (Job 32:6-9).
- He withholds his opinion until everyone else has finished (Job 32:10-11).
- He refuses to take personal insult at Job's defense (Job 32:14).
- He is committed to speaking in kindness, without accusation (Job 33:2-7).
- He will respond to Job's words rather than terrifying him (Job 33:8-11).
- He will defend God (Job 33:12).

Elihu builds a four-part defense of God and his ways. We will look at an early section because it touches on issues that Job and his friends have discussed already. Elihu says,

> "For God speaks in one way,
> and in two, though man does not perceive it.
> In a dream, in a vision of the night,

when deep sleep falls on men,
      while they slumber on their beds,
then he opens the ears of men
      and terrifies them with warnings,
that he may turn man aside from his deed
      and conceal pride from a man;
he keeps his soul from the pit,
      his life from perishing by the sword....

"Behold, God does all these things,
      twice, three times, with a man,
to bring back his soul from the pit,
      that he may be lighted with the light of life."

—Job 33:14-18, 29-30, emphasis added.

Elihu's description of nightmarish warnings probably stands in response to the nightmare scene in Eliphaz's first speech. Where Eliphaz intended to terrify, Elihu eliminates the graphic details and brings a much more positive message. God wants to get our attention so he can rescue us from destruction.

Elihu's contention is partly, but not entirely, correct. According to Elihu, God brings crises *so that* we will seek him. We witnessed the truth of his words on 9/11, during the Sandy Hook school shootings, and in the Boston Marathon bombing. When crises occur, people do turn to God. But this is not the only reason that God allows evil to exist. Walton and Longman offer this excellent observation on the presence of evil in the world.

> Rather than following our natural inclination to evaluate these evidences as a sign of God's weakness, negligence or capriciousness, we should see this approach as a result of his grace. If the cosmos were to be brought into total conformity to justice, there would be no room for sinners—forgiven or otherwise. Instead love constrains him, and we are recipients of his mercy in unknown and uncounted ways.[15]

Part of the answer to Rabbi Kushner's dilemma arises from his assumption that "God wants the righteous to live peaceful, happy lives."[16] In truth, God cares far more about our eternal souls than about our momentary comfort. As human beings we are unable to understand the mechanics behind the many momentary crises we face. But by comparison, crisis is far better than eternal destruction.

Journal Entry

In your suffering, have others treated you as a problem to be fixed? What do you see wrong with their approach? _____

_____

_____

This chapter briefly discussed Job's understanding of justice. Everyone who suffers struggles with these issues. What are your feelings about justice and God's relationship with you at this moment? _____

_____

_____

Elihu, the young man who concluded the dialogues, defended God's goodness in his performance of justice. Do you know anyone like Elihu, whom you can trust to guide you wisely? What kind of perspective can his words put on your difficulty? _____

_____

_____

CHAPTER 3

Job and the Problem of Suffering, Part 2: God's Answer to the Problem of Evil

But he knows the way that I take;
when he has tried me, I shall come out as gold.
—Job 23:10

The LORD's Appearance to Job

As we press through the book of Job, the human voices become silent. Eliphaz, Bildad, and Zophar relinquish their attacks on Job, convinced that the task is futile. Job declares his speeches are finished. And Elihu completes his defense of God's goodness.

Then, the book turns. God appears and gives Job the audience he has demanded. Appropriately, he speaks from a whirlwind (Job 38:1). We do not know whether this is only a high wind or an actual tornado. We can be sure that his appearance is terrifying because his speech to Job is frightening. The LORD's opening words are ominous.

"Who is this that darkens counsel by words without
    knowledge?
Dress for action like a man;
    I will question you, and you make it known to me...."

—Job 38:2-3

God's Shock and Awe approach is purposeful. C.S. Lewis writes, "God whispers to us in our pleasures, speaks in our conscience, but shouts in our pain: it is His megaphone to rouse a deaf world."[17] In Job, God's megaphone

28

has become a ship's horn. If the call were any louder, it would blow out Job's eardrums.

The Prerequisite for the Big Questions

For four chapters (Job 38-41) God pummels Job with demands, which all have the same form: "If you think you can do the heavy lifting, show me that you have mastered the light stuff first."

Of course, Job cannot. The man who tried to post his credentials as an expert witness concerning justice in the universe discovers he first must be able to answer the questions about the cosmos itself. In other words, he cannot challenge the "why" questions until he can answer the "what" questions.

Part One of the Interrogations: Questions Regarding Creation, (Job 38:1-40:5)

God's first challenge concerns the nature of the cosmos. If Job wants God to apologize about matters of justice in the world, then Job needs to be able to explain the nature of the world itself. He begins,

> "Where were you when I laid the foundations of the
> earth?
> Tell me, if you have understanding.
> Who determined its measurements—surely you know!"

> —Job 38:4-5a

The interrogation moves through the physical universe and into the biological realm.

> "Can you hunt the prey for the lion,
> or satisfy the appetite of the young lions....?"

> "Who provides for the raven its prey,
> when its young ones cry to God for help,
> and wander about for lack of food?

Do you know when the mountain goats give birth?
Do you observe the calving of the does?...

"Who has let the wild donkey go free?
Who has loosed the bonds of the swift donkey,
to whom I have given the arid plain for his home
and the salt land for his dwelling place?"
—Job 38:39, 41; 39:1, 5-6

For two chapters God pummels Job with questions concerning the creation. Job is unable to answer them. He has neither the understanding to comprehend the physical world nor the ability to determine order in the biosphere. The section ends with a concluding challenge from God and a confession of inadequacy from Job.

And the LORD said to Job:

"Shall a faultfinder contend with the Almighty?
He who argues with God, let him answer it."

Then Job answered the LORD and said:

"Behold, I am of small account; what shall I answer you?
I lay my hand on my mouth.
I have spoken once, and I will not answer;
twice, but I will proceed no further."

—Job 40:1-5

Part Two of the Interrogation: Questions on Justice, (Job 40:6-42:6)

Job may be ready to cry, "Uncle!" but God means to take the fight all the way to the end. The theodicy question, the issue over which Job has insisted his understanding exceeds God's, comes next. Job has challenged God's credibility as Supreme Judge of the cosmos, and God means to defend his position. The issue is either black or white. If God has acted unjustly toward

Job, then he owes Job an apology. But if Job has spoken presumptuously, then he must answer for his hasty words.

The first part of the interrogation sets the qualifying rules to be able to stand as Creator. The position requires the complete understanding of the cosmos and biosphere, a human impossibility. The second section involves an even more difficult task, the administration of justice in the cosmos. The prerequisite for donning the chief justice's robe is majesty. The opening volley in the second section introduces the LORD in his power as Judge.

> Then the LORD answered Job out of the whirlwind and
>   said:
>
> "Dress for action like a man;
>   I will question you, and you make it known to me.
> Will you even put me in the wrong?
>   Will you condemn me that you may be in the right?
> Have you an arm like God,
>   and can you thunder with a voice like his?
>
> "Adorn yourself with majesty and dignity;
>   clothe yourself with glory and splendor.
> Pour out the overflowing of your anger,
>   and look on everyone who is proud and abase him.
> Look on everyone who is proud and bring him low
>   and tread down the wicked where they stand.
> Hide them all in the dust together;
>   bind their faces in the world below.
> Then will I also acknowledge to you
>   that your own right hand can save you."

—Job 40:6-14

The line of reasoning in this section involves the fundamental nature of justice, a point that Job has lost in his confusion. Job has thought he could elevate himself to an advisory capacity before God. He believed he could tell God a thing or two about justice.

But rather than being the outcome of a consensus by a board of advisors, justice is unilateral. In a game of cosmic King of the Hill, only one person can stand on the top of the hill. If Job wishes to justify himself, he can do so only by taking God's place as chief justice. God says, "Will you even put me in the wrong? / Will you condemn me that you may be in the right?" (Job 40:8).

Sometimes jealousy is a good thing, and God has a right to be jealous in his title. He owns it by his nature. Justice is not an abstract principle that God uses to gauge his actions. He does not become "just" in the sense that he measures up to an external standard.

Instead, justice is the purpose to which God engages himself. He adorns himself in "majesty and dignity," and clothes himself in "glory and splendor" to judge (Job 40:10). The terms depict purpose. We will discuss this idea in more detail in our study of Psalm 9/10 Chapter 6.

The Just and All-powerful God

If we reconsider the college student's challenge at the beginning of this book, we find that two new factors bear on his argument. The first involves the meaning of "good" in the statement, "A good God would want to prevent evil." The student's use of the word misses the biblical concept of majesty. It implies a gentle old man who would love to make the world a warm, fuzzy place. The biblical God is far different. The biblical God is the righteous God who *must* judge evil. His self-proclaimed reason for being is to carry out justice in the world. God has every intention to carry out his role as Judge.

The same goes for the student's second statement, "An all-powerful God would be able to prevent evil." A proper understanding of Job will call us to acknowledge God's authority rather than challenging it. This statement is essentially a repeat of Job's argument. Both Job and the student reason in the same terms. If God *refuses* to prevent evil, then he must be *unable* to stop evil.

However, the God we see in Job is an all-powerful God who uses evil against itself to achieve greater ends. He also is committed to rectify evil and bring it to an end so that justice reigns. God is not a kindhearted old man who wishes he could just make everybody share the sandbox. He is majestic. He thunders with his voice, overflows with anger, abases the proud and brings them low, and treads down the wicked where they stand

(Job 40:11-14). This understanding of God's justice forms the bedrock basis for the faith that propels the psalms of lament.

Majesty

As God prepares to close his interrogation of Job, he takes us into the confluence of authority, goodness, and purpose. In his final words to Job, he focuses on two majestic animals: Behemoth (Job 40:15-24), and Leviathan (Job 41:1-34). The Hebrew word for *animal* is *behema*. The plural of majesty for *behema* is *Behemoth* and means "Great Animal." The description of Behemoth depicts a large wetlands creature. Without preamble, the LORD tells Job,

> "Behold Behemoth,
>> which I made as I made you.
>> he eats grain like an ox.
> Behold, his strength is in his loins,
>> and his power in the muscles of his belly.
> He makes his tail stiff like a cedar,
>> the sinews of his thighs are knit together.
> His bones are like tubes of bronze,
>> his limbs like bars of iron
> He is first in the works of God;
>> let him who made him bring near his sword!...
>
> Behold, if the river is turbulent he is not frightened;
>> he is confident though Jordan rushes against his mouth."

—Job 40:15-19, 23

Behemoth showcases God's creative prowess as "first in the works of God" (Job 40:19).

The account moves directly from Behemoth to Leviathan (Job 41:1-34), a descriptive section that takes up three times the space that Behemoth does. Leviathan (another transliterated name) is a powerful armored sea creature that resists harpoons and spears (Job 41:7), and apparently is impossible to capture. The account begins with a description of the monster itself.

> "Can you draw out Leviathan with a fishhook
> or press down his tongue with a cord?
> Can you put a rope in his nose
> or pierce his jaw with a hook...?"

—Job 41:1-2

As the case is with Behemoth, the majesty behind Leviathan lies in its power. In the middle of the description, however, the LORD interjects the rhetorical connection to his right to judge. The line of comparison moves from Leviathan to the God who created him:

> "Behold, the hope of a man is false [before Leviathan];
> he is laid low even at the sight of him.
> No one is so fierce that he dares to stir him up.
> *Who then is he who can stand before me, that I should repay him?*
> Whatever is under the whole heaven is mine."

—Job 41:9-11, emphasis added

The comparison is straightforward. If Leviathan, a created being, is so fierce, "Who then is he who can stand before me...?" (Job 41:10). Job would never presume to go toe to toe with Behemoth or Leviathan in their majesty. How does he presume to lecture the God who created them? If we include the interlude, God's description of Leviathan moves through thirty-four verses. Leviathan closes God's defense. God has shown that he alone possesses the understanding, authority, and majesty to handle the problems that evil brings into the world.

The Problem of Evil for the Skeptic

Questions about the nature of evil in the world are permissible. Both skeptics and believers ask them. The college student, a self-declared atheist, thought he had tied down the answer. According to the student, evil is simultaneously a fact of life and proof positive that God cannot exist. Following his opening syllogism, he wrote the following commentary:

1. God is by definition omniscient, omnipotent, and omni-benevolent [sic].
2. If God is all-powerful, he *can* prevent evil.
3. If God is all-knowing, he *knows how* to prevent evil
4. If God is good, he *wants* to prevent evil.
5. But since there is evil, God cannot exist.

The student's in-your-face statement against God hung on his door throughout the school year until summer break. When he posted it again the following fall, I decided the time had come to speak up. I wrote a reply and taped it to the wall beside his door. The response read,

A Reply: The Reality of Transcendence

The reality of transcendence answers the problem of evil by showing God's rule over the enemies who oppose him:

1. *Evil* is defined in moral terms.
2. Moral terms are defined by their relationship to a *transcendent God*, one who gives meaning to the cosmos from outside the cosmos.
3. If God does not exist, then *moral meaning* cannot exist.
4. If moral meaning does not exist, then *evil* cannot be defined.
5. Since the world is ruled by material causes within a closed system, nothing can be evil. What is, is right.

The God of the Scripture created the cosmos, set Adam at the head of creation, and provided him a moral framework in which he would operate. Instead of depriving Adam of moral choice, he gave him the opportunity to prove his loyalty in a simple test. Adam had complete liberty to enjoy everything in the Garden, and was prohibited only from a single fruit.

The fact that Adam chose evil over what was right implies neither God's impotence nor surprise. Instead, God revealed that he would abolish the problem of evil personally, through his Son, Jesus Christ. His death and resurrection in history show once for all that God would tear down the wall that separates evil human beings from his favor. He answered the dilemma of evil—how a good God can bring sinful people into his presence—by Christ's substitution on the cross. Jesus took the heat for our sin and gave us his perfect righteousness in its place if we but receive the gift.

I included my name and contact information at the bottom of my reply, and invited the student to discuss the ideas further if he wished. He did not answer, but that does not matter. The point is less about the argument than it is to know how we seek God in his glory when all other options have vanished.

The Problem of Control

Though he failed to realize the fact, the student's challenge ultimately proved to be shortsighted. Suppose we lived in a world in which God had prevented evil, in thought and deed. Suppose that God had flipped a switch that turned off any possibility for us to conceive or carry out evil against him.

The consequences are obvious. If God had made evil thoughts or actions impermissible, then we as his subjects would lack any ability to do wrong or even to think questioning thoughts. Our only conceivable emotion toward God would be adoration. Do you see the problem with this picture? No one would think to call our worship "love," because love is something that grows internally, often in the midst of great pain. Love signifies a deepening relationship that overcomes difficulties. Any adoration we might feel in a universe devoid of all evil would be sterile and monochromatic.

Loyalty would be a fiction as well because the word's definition implies dedication in the midst of opposing interests. Even the notion of righteousness and justice would become suspect. By definition, justice means the righting of wrongs. In a world in which all evil is impossible, justice would be no more conceivable than the fourth dimension. Similarly, "righteousness" would mean nothing more than conformity to our preprogramming.

A God who prevents all evil in the world just because he can is a God who ultimately is too afraid to deal with opposition. He would be a God who created a dystopia in which everything and everyone lay under his direct control.

The Believer and the Question of God's Authority

What about Rabbi Kushner's alternative, a God who would like to address the evil in the world, but ultimately lacks the power to do so? In Chapter 2 we discussed his observations on people's common assumptions regarding God's power. Here again are the assumptions that most people make about God, humanity, and their place in the cosmos:

A. God is all-powerful and causes everything that happens in the world. Nothing happens without His willing it.
B. God is just and fair, and stands for people getting what they deserve, so that the good prosper and the wicked are punished.
C. Job is a good person.[18]

Rabbi Kushner concluded that Statement A., "God is all-powerful," has to be false. In his words, "Forced to choose between a good God who is not totally powerful, or a powerful God who is not fully good, the author of Job chooses to believe in God's goodness....God wants the righteous to live peaceful, happy lives, but sometimes even He can't bring that about.[19]

In the book of Job, we see a different reality altogether. After the divine interrogation, Job the man concludes,

> "I know that you can do all things,
>   and that no purpose of yours can be thwarted."

—Job 42:2

Job's conclusion is the opposite of Kushner's. God, in fact, is all-powerful. Nothing in the book of Job suggests that God ever has lost control over his universe. He handles the problem of evil in a radically different manner than we would anticipate, and ultimately brings an even greater degree of goodness from evil.

To acknowledge God's proper station as ruler of the cosmos, we need to rethink Rabbi Kushner's ideas on fairness and goodness. We will affirm the truth of the first statement, and will leave it as he wrote it. However, we must restate propositions B. and C.

A. (As stated by Rabbi Kushner): God is all-powerful and causes everything that happens in the world. Nothing happens without His willing it.

B. (Revised from Rabbi Kushner): God is just, and stands for justice in uprightness. He will vindicate the oppressed and bring the wicked to justice (see Psalm 9:7-8). Sometimes God accomplishes the task during this life. Even if he delays, however, he will bring justice to the earth, both in granting restitution to the innocent and in bringing just punishment to the wicked.

C. (Revised from Rabbi Kushner): The introduction to the book of Job describes Job as "blameless and upright, one who feared God and turned away from evil" (Job 1:1). In other words, he is a good man insofar as he honors his Creator. But he still lacks the authority to demand God to prevent evil from happening to him. Job himself acknowledges that he cannot stand before God's ultimate goodness. In the end, no one can stand before the Lord and demand acceptance by God. We live because God is gracious, not because of anything we have done to deserve life.

Finally, to close the circle in our reasoning, we will add a fourth statement to the three we have borrowed from Rabbi Kushner:

D. The fact that God is all-powerful does not mean he lacks concern for human suffering. He seeks to establish deeper relationships with the people he loves, because he desires a deeper and richer relationship with us. God wants us to know *him* personally. To do so, he has chosen to suffer with us. The greatest example of divine suffering—and the most significant proof that he cares for us—comes from Jesus Christ himself, who came to earth as the

Son of God, suffered throughout his life, and ultimately sacrificed himself in agony.

In the book of Job, the big picture becomes the key to understanding the details. Job demanded to have a say in the details of his life when he had no way to understand the whole. His demand was more than he could handle. In the end, he did not need to try.

For example, if we want to build safe suspension bridges, we need to master the most rigorous design and engineering principles. Only a few engineers in the world attain this level of expertise. But if we want to drive across them safely, we need only to get into our vehicle and go. We do not need to know the structural design principles of the bridges we cross, because we can trust the builder.

Likewise, we could never hope to understand all the ways that good and evil interact in our lives. We only need to know that we can trust the God who can do all things. If he can create and sustain the cosmos, and bring justice in majesty, he can handle our most difficult moral questions.

The End of Job

The last chapter in Job contains a short epilog to round out the prolog in chapters 1-2. Ironically, Job never learns about the cosmic conflict that imposed such a high level of tension through the rest of the book. The struggle for his soul remains concealed. Were he able to know about it, his knowledge would have led to pride.

Think about the Eliphaz's first speech, however. He confidently maintained that God never would be able to trust unfaithful mortals. Yet that is what God did when he allowed Satan to attack Job. The only reason God gave Satan such wide latitude was to show Job's trust to the world. God allowed Satan to take Job though cruel suffering because he knew Job's heart. Yes, Job stumbled, but in the end, he repented.

Job, in turn, learns more about than he would have if God had prevented the evil from occurring to him. Now, he receives a vision of God in his glory. His final recorded words are,

> "I had heard of you by the hearing of the ear,
>   but now my eye sees you;

> therefore I despise myself,
> and repent in dust and ashes."

—Job 42:5-6

Job realizes his greatest blessing does not lie in knowing *what* or *why*. It comes from knowing God.

Ironically, Job's physical healing grows out of his breaking. Immediately after Job states his confession, the LORD turns to Eliphaz. His words are ominous.

> The LORD said to Eliphaz the Temanite: "My anger burns against you and against your two friends, for you have not spoken of me what is right, as my servant Job has. Now therefore take seven bulls and seven rams and go to my servant Job and offer up a burnt offering for yourselves. And my servant Job shall pray for you, for I will accept his prayer not to deal with you according to your folly. For you have not spoken of me what is right, as my servant Job has."

—Job 7-8

For years I believed that Job's right speaking of the LORD had to do with his superior theology. I have come to the conclusion that such a position is impossible. Even though Job's early theology is more insightful than his friends' beliefs, it still suffers from the same defects. Therefore, the only alternative for Job's right speaking lies in his confession. There he speaks truth. Job has uttered things too wonderful for him to understand.

God accepts his repentance. His acceptance shows what grace means. Even though Job has slandered God, in the end, God considers only his confession. The man emerges as clean as fresh snow.

In the final paragraphs of the book, the LORD restores Job's fortunes to twice their previous level—14,000 sheep, 6,000 camels, 1,000 yokes of oxen, and 1,000 donkeys. Then the Scripture adds a curious verse. "He had also seven sons and three daughters" (Job 42:13), a number equal to the children he had lost.

Why not fourteen sons and six daughters?

40

Let me explain with an example. When I volunteered at a local Hospice, I worked with a bereavement group for parents who had lost children. The difficulties in facing the loss of a child are complex. The child is gone, but a dynamic presence remains in the hopes and expectations for the child's future. The parents mourn what would have been the first date, graduation, engagement, marriage, and other milestones. At the same time, the lost child forever remains frozen at the same age. No new pictures or memories replace the old ones.

Most people are unaware of these dynamics, and often this leads to deep hurt. Recently one of the members told the group that one of the cruelest things anyone had ever made was the comment, "I don't know why you're so sad. You can always have another child."

The member responded in anger. "I will never be able to replace my child." He was right. We do not "get over" that kind of loss, and we certainly should not expect any new children we may have to "replace" the ones who have passed.

Children are not possessions. They are family, and the Bible understands this. Though Job and his wife had lost their first ten children, the children remained a part of the household. The couple would remain the parents of fourteen sons and six daughters. Living or dead, they were still their children. Therefore, when God gives them ten more children, he has given him double. The first ten are with the Lord, but they never will be forgotten.

Conclusion

The end of Job is as significant for what it leaves out as it is in what it affirms. As much as the book reveals, it still leaves a host of specific "why" questions unanswered.

- Why do the wicked prosper while the righteous suffer?
- Why do bad things happen to good people?
- Why do evil people get away with murder?
- Why does God allow evil to continue in the world?

When life pummels us, we find ourselves in much the same position as Job—ignorant of the details and crying for satisfaction. God is not silent because he is incapable of answering. He remains silent because we are not able to balance evil against good. We cannot clothe ourselves in majesty and bring justice into the cosmos.

Ultimately God directs us to find our satisfaction in knowing him rather than ferreting out the answers. This fact does not mean we must go through life with our fingers in our ears while we sing, "Tra-la-la." As we will see in the next section, the Psalms show us how to wrestle with God over the issues that crush us. The collection of addresses along the path from mourning to praise will teach us to grieve God's way.

Journal Entry

The difficulties we face can become overwhelming. First, write out the details of the situation you face. How does it threaten you? What are you afraid might happen?

_____

_____

_____

_____

Second, how do you think a grounded awareness of God's ultimate power over evil may be able to help you face your particular situation? (This question should not be, "How can God get me out of this?" Instead, it should be, "How can I learn to develop a greater appreciation of God *through* this?)

_____

_____

_____

_____

PART 2

EMPLOYING THE PSALMS OF LAMENT

CHAPTER 4

The Psalms: Letters from the Front

Whoever sings songs to a heavy heart
is like one who takes off a garment on a cold day,
and like vinegar on soda.
—Proverbs 25:20

Food for Our Soul's Deepest Desire

A few weeks after my wife Marie died, a long-time work friend and her husband invited me to visit their church and then to share dinner with them. I welcomed both. I belonged to a small church with a young pastor, and I grieved alone. My friends attended a much larger church. The invitation to join them offered me an opportunity to enjoy a brief time of anonymity, and, I hoped, a greater depth of worship and teaching from a larger faith community. I wanted to be able to seek God's face with tears. I also knew that my friends' dinner invitation was genuine. They would allow me to relax without feeling any pressure to conform.

The time with my friends was priceless. They understood my situation. They let me share stories and asked for nothing in return. Their ministry to me that day was one of the kindest acts that anyone has shown me. I will never forget their act of kindness.

The church experience turned out to be another story.

At the beginning of the service, a band began with praise choruses. After several of these—during which I found myself unable to sing—the stage cleared. A young woman stepped up and began a soliloquy, lamenting the loss of the hymns that once had graced her church. She longed for the old days when the church rang with music that was meaningful to *her*.

I happen to be one who loves hymnody, and I found myself drawn to the young lady's words. She spoke my language. I waited for the high praise that was to follow.

As events turned out, my wait was in vain. In mid-homily, a man entered and confronted her. I realized that what I thought was a speech was part of a moralistic skit, and the character with whom I had identified was the designated fall-girl.

The two argued their points back and forth, although the dialogue lacked any logical progression from one subject to the next. Instead, the text served only to establish the man's point. In a few short lines, the moral weight shifted from the first character's defense for the hymns to the other character's pronouncement. Roll over, Beethoven. Hymnody is dead, and we are here to praise. The young lady never had a chance to say another substantive word.

Once the pronouncement ended, the praise team took over the stage once again. The church sang one more chorus. Then the band cleared, and the speaker, the same man who had silenced the woman during the skit, took the stand. He introduced himself as the worship leader. The head pastor happened to be on vacation that week and had asked his music guy to do the sermon. As the praise leader, he had chosen to present his defense for—you guessed it—praise music. His lesson consisted of three points, and went something like this:

- First, people criticize the worship choruses because they cannot equal the old hymns. They argue that the choruses lack content when compared to the old material. Well, two hundred years ago, people said the same thing when the new hymns began to replace their old hymns, so the argument must be invalid.
- Second, instead of trying to hold on to out-of-date models, we need to ask more direct questions. For example, was the worship pleasing to the Lord? Of course, it was. Case closed.
- Therefore, nothing is wrong. Praise music is here to stay, and the audience needs to get with the program.

I chafed in my mind. I had come to the church to mourn. My heart ached to worship in a way that was both biblical and relevant to my present situation. Instead, I felt like the song leader had shoved praise in my face. I left with questions. Was I wrong because I needed to grieve? Did I spoil the party because I was unable to laugh with the crowd? I wondered why I felt so victimized by someone less than half my age.

To be fair to the other side, I occupied the distinct minority. Most of the audience had come to praise. The church's collective heart desired to worship in a way that was both biblical and relevant to their present situation. They were as justified in their need to praise as I was in my need to mourn. Both praise and mourning were appropriate.

Over time I came to understand the situation more objectively. My grief was only part of the reason I reacted so negatively. The music leader's presentation was shoddy. He rushed through hasty conclusions because he knew his arguments would be unable to endure rigorous examination. He probably was unable to recognize the legitimacy of grief or to connect the logical dots between pain and worship from a broken heart.

I cannot fault him for his omission. He was young and zealous. At the same time, he answered to a higher calling than he understood at the time. Worship is more than praise alone. I have to hope he has done the hard work since that time and has begun to understand the reality and blessedness of mourning.

Connecting the Dots between Mourning and Praise

How can we practice both mourning and praise in worship without looking like we are trying to mix water and gasoline?

The short answer is this. We need to understand the bipolar nature of mourning and praise from a biblical perspective. In physics, we cannot have a magnetic north without a corresponding magnetic south. Nor can we have a biblical understanding of praise without an understanding of its opposite pole, grief.

Praise has its place in biblical worship, but the Psalms never call for words of praise in isolation from everything else. Praise draws its deepest meaning as an expression of deliverance from situations that formerly called for lament. The Psalms offer praise *because* the LORD has brought the writers out of situations that have caused them grief. Old Testament scholar Claus Westermann offers this insight.

> In Israel all speaking to God moved between these two poles [petition and praise]. There is no petition, no

pleading from the depths, that did not know at least one step (in looking back to God's earlier saving activity or in confession of confidence) on the road to praise. *But there is also no praise that was fully separated from the experience of God's wonderful intervention in the time of need, none that had become a mere stereotyped liturgy.*[20]

The First Pole: Pleading from the Depths

Praise in the Psalms never exists for itself. Psalms of orientation laud God for who he is and what he does, but these reflect the experiential journey from mourning to praise. They understand that they are the endpoint of a voyage that has begun in grief. The writers remember the depths because that is the place where they took up the cry to God to rescue them. In a real way, the psalms of lament are letters from the front, sent back home in the hope that we ultimately may return with songs of deliverance.

To understand the journey from mourning to praise more fully, we need to consider three aspects of grief and loss. These are grief, mourning, and lament.

- *Grief* is the pain that occurs when our world collapses or turns against us. One author describes it as "embodied anguish."[21] Grief is the natural reaction when we lose something deeply meaningful. It is a universal human emotion. On the one hand, it is far bigger than we are. It knocks us down and holds us under its control. It carries us along and pummels us, leaving us to wonder whether we will feel anything other than grief again. But even with its great power over us, we can resist. We often deny grief's presence. Such a practice is never healthy, but it does not change the fact that we do it. Our denial does not erase our pain, but it does allow us to suppress it, at least for a time.
- *Mourning* is doing grief out loud. When we mourn, we make a statement in our pain. In contrast to grief, mourning is active and undeniable. Our pain has come to the surface, and we no longer

can deny it. However, mourning may or may not be purposeful. Mourning has just as much power to carry us along as grief does.

- *Lament* occurs when we direct our grief toward God as a deliberate act of worship. Lament is just as tragic, just as painful, and just as sharp as grief or mourning, but it is active, conscious, and purposeful. When we perform lament in a biblical manner, we direct our sorrow toward God as a prayer. Lament is a call to God to deliver us from our pain.

The psalms of lament always focus on a plea to God to act. In broad brushstrokes, the psalms of lament follow this general structure:

Address (and introductory petition)
Lament or complaint
Turning toward God (confession of trust)
Petition
Vow of praise[22]

In this model, the *address* is the section where the psalmist calls out to God. It is his first cry for help.

The *lament* forms the complaint before God. It can be a cry for help against the psalmist's enemies, a plea for God to extend mercy during a time of anger, or a confession of remorse.

Turning toward God is the act by which the psalmist confesses his confidence in God and his faithfulness.

The *petition* is the specific request. One of the most common petitions in the Psalms calls for God to bring justice into an unjust situation.

The *vow of praise* occurs in almost every lament in Scripture. In this book, the vow of praise will be one of our most important concepts. It is far deeper than a promise to savor feelings of thankfulness. It is the pledge to acknowledge God publically for rescuing the writer. This was especially important in ancient culture because people identified with their family or clan. Therefore, the vow of praise signified the intent to offer a public invitation to celebrate God's deliverance. Westermann writes,

> For primitive man an attitude does not exist except in its expression, for man does not exist "in himself," but only in community with other men (the Hebrew *'ādām*

means "mankind")....In the place of sacrifice the Psalms placed praise and obedience, not an attitude, but activity directed toward God....Where a worshiper in the Psalms says, "I will praise the Lord...," he does not mean, "I will be thankful to God," but, "I will respond to him for what he has done for me."[23]

When David writes in Psalm 22, a psalm of lament, I will tell of your name to my brothers; / in the midst of the congregation I will praise you (Psalm 22:22), he has this relationship with his people in mind. Praise is the public fulfillment of the vow, and the result is responsive:

> You who fear the LORD, praise him!
> All you offspring of Jacob, glorify him,
>   and stand in awe of him, all you offspring of Israel!
>
> —Psalm 22:23

The psalmists raise their voices to God because they know that God is capable of correcting the situation, whether it involves restoration to a previous station in life, vengeance against enemies, or forgiveness of sin. The psalms of lament address both of the questions we raised in the first part of this book. They believe God *can* make things right because they know he is all-powerful. And they know with equal certainty that he *will* make them right because he is good. For this reason, laments are acts of worship expressed as confessions of trust. The psalmists believe that God ultimately will deliver them from their difficulties and restore them to a place where they again can offer praise.

The Second Pole: Praise from the Heights

Praise in the Psalms always praises God *for* something, either who he is or what he does. The Psalms exalt both God's character and works. But they understand God's character through the witness of his works. God is good because he has done good things on the writers' behalf. He is praiseworthy because of what he has done. A substantial majority of praise psalms are declarative (telling what God has done) rather than descriptive (praising

God for who he is). [24] That is, they look back to particular instances of deliverance and call for the congregation to rejoice with the writers.

Praise, then, is the capstone of the Psalms, not its cornerstone. Praise in the Psalms reaches back to the lament from which it has risen. Lament gives depth to adoration.

For example, Psalm 149 is a psalm of descriptive praise. It can be summarized by the statements, "God is..." or "God does...." It begins with a call to praise in general terms but soon moves to the reason for praise. Here is the beginning:

> Praise the LORD!
> Sing to the LORD a new song,
>> his praise in the assembly of the godly!
> Let Israel be glad in his Maker;
>> let the children of Zion rejoice in their King!
> Let them praise his name with dancing,
>> making melody to him with tambourine and lyre!
>
> —Psalm 149:1-3

The next line gives the reason for praise, a general description of what he does.

> For the LORD takes pleasure in his people;
>> he adorns the humble with salvation.
>
> —Psalm 149:4

Descriptive praise like this occurs in only a few of the praise psalms. Most of the praises refer to particular works. In broad terms, they declare, "I will praise God because he has acted this way on my behalf...." These are declarative psalms. For example, Psalm 116, the subject of Chapter 11, begins with these words:

> I love the LORD, because he has heard
>> my voice and my pleas for mercy.
> Because he inclined his ear to me,
>> therefore I will call on him as long as I live.

The snares of death encompassed me,
the pangs of Sheol [or the grave] laid hold on me;
I suffered distress and anguish.
Then I called on the name of the LORD:
"O LORD, I pray, deliver my soul!"

—Psalm 116:1-4

The prayer is simple. Before God's rescue, the psalmist was a dead man walking. When he called on God to deliver him, God responded. The writer's praise draws meaning from the fact that it remembers the depths from which it came. It celebrates the journey from tragedy to deliverance.

In simple terms, lament and praise coexist. Lament is worship. A cry to God out of our depths is just as much an act of faith as a song of praise. Lament represents a genuine faith response to a real life situation. Lament holds grief and praise in tension. On the one hand, it tells God, "I will wait for you," while on the other it cries out in impatience, "How long, O LORD...?"

Job, the Psalms, and the Line We Dare Not Cross

We have one more point to make. On the surface, the Psalms bear a strong resemblance to Job. Many of the grievances in the book sound like Job's complaints. Conversely, many of the passages in Job that magnify God are very doxological and resemble the language in the Psalms.

Under the surface, however, the difference between Job and the Psalms becomes significant. The Psalms in particular stand on the believer's covenant relationship with his or her God. They do so rightly. Regardless of where we live in history, we have incredible privileges in our relationship with our God. The psalms of lament capitalize on the believers' right to have a voice before the LORD.

At the same time, the Psalms also understand that God is holy and that his holiness has a bearing on the way we approach him. If we understand the Bible's high view of God, we can imagine a line in the Bible that says, "Worship stops where self-exaltation begins." When Job tried to argue his self-righteousness as an actual quality before the LORD, he crossed the self-exaltation line. The Psalms avoid that error, even when the laments become accusatory.

The difference between Job and the psalms of lament lies in the way each approaches the language. Job tried to use accusatory language objectively against God. The psalms of lament limit their accusations to the feelings of the person seeking an audience with God. The Psalms complain loudly, but they stay on the side of the line that recognizes that God is God and we are not.

> The question, "How long?" just as the question "Why?" asks about the absence of God. In them verbs of anger predominate.
>
> Beside these accusatory questions are complaints in the form of statements....They tread that thin line between reproach and judgment. But never do they condemn God, for the utterances are never objective statements. They always remain personal address.[25]

Continuing in this Book

I have selected the psalms in this section of the book because of the variety of situations they address. They are arranged to trace the journey from mourning to praise. As you read them, you will observe different grieving situations and various stages of grief along your voyage. The psalms in this section are meant to be way stations on your journey back to praise. Psalm 88 will even address despair (yes, God allows us to say, "I have lost all hope"). They will not leave you there, however. After the chapter on Psalm 88, the studies will concentrate on the journey back to praise, which culminates in Psalm 116, a meditation on fulfilling the vow of praise. My hope is that they will assist you in your journey.

Chapter 5

Psalm 13

Establishing our Personal Spiritual Narrative

"If all experienced God in the same way, and returned Him an identical worship, the song of the Church triumphant would have no symphony, it would be like an orchestra in which all the instruments played the same note."[26]

Easy Theology and Spiritual Finger Pointing

During the 1990's, Christian message billboards became popular. With solid black backgrounds and short messages printed in white, the messages were usually well thought out. One that I saw failed. It read, "If God seems distant, guess who moved." The message was humorless, accusatory, and lacking in any redemptive value. Rather than inviting the reader to consider a way to open a dialogue with God, it hurled condemnation. We almost can sense Job's three friends lurking behind the billboard, whispering in unison, "If you suffer because of __(fill in the blank)__, it must be your fault."

Theology like this appears to be self-evident. It is also dangerously wrong. I bring this example to the study of Psalm 13 because it stands so far from sound biblical reasoning. It denies one of the deepest tenets in the Psalms: God cares.

How, then, can we separate the good theology from error? Primarily, by reading carefully. Close reading takes work, but the discipline is worth developing.

Even though the billboard makes a theological statement regarding our personal relationship to God, the real driving force is the narrative that runs beneath the surface. The story builds the sense of reality through which the theology gains its meaning. Before our theology ever appears on the page, the narrative creates the universe where the belief lives.

Have you ever engaged in an argument with a person who just *knows* he is right? Even when you present all the facts to him, he refuses to budge. The reason is simple. Facts alone are unable to persuade. The person's personal narrative, the way he interprets the world, is the driving force behind his understanding of events. He can believe something that appears contradictory to another person because his narrative causes him to interpret the facts in a way that maintains self-consistency.

Narrative as Story

A narrative is a story, and story weaves itself into our being. We may meet people who say they avoid fiction, but fiction is only a small part of story. Engage anyone in conversation about anything, and you soon will find yourself sharing personal stories.

In the Bible, half of the Old Testament and almost two-thirds of the New Testament are narrative. A good story gives us a sense of fulfillment when we finish it because the characters meet the conflict on their terms, deal with it in a manner that is appropriate to the story setting, and bring about a believable and satisfying resolution.

If we reduce any story to its simplest terms, we find three elements. Aristotle called them a beginning, middle, and end.[27] His full development is beyond the scope of this book, but for our purposes, we can describe the elements this way:

- Beginning: A conflict that develops when characters' interests clash
- Middle: Escalation of the conflict to the point where a confrontation must occur
- End: Resolution of the conflict

The Story Behind the Billboard Theology

The seven words on the billboard contain all three story elements. We have to dig to find them, but they are present in the narrative. Unfortunately, they are one-dimensional.

- **Beginning—Characters in conflict**

  The billboard begins with two characters. One is God. The other is the reader, which we can describe as an understood "you." The conflict involves a breakdown in the two-character relationship, described by the words, "If God seems distant." That is, if he seems distant to you.

- **Middle—Escalation and confrontation**

  In the billboard writers' world, life is simple. The mere existence of the conflict receives its answer in the three words, "Guess who moved." In contrast to a flesh-and-blood clash that can escalate or diminish, the degree of conflict is irrelevant in this story. The conflict just is. The entire problem exists because you, the reader, must have moved.

- **End—Resolution**

  For a story resolution to be satisfying, it has to address the conflict in a way that respects its terms. The end may be unexpected, but when we look back at the development in the story, we can trace the logical steps from the beginning to the end. The billboard narration lacks this element. The finger-pointing conclusion says nothing about cause, escalation, or resolution. It is just a morality tale in seven words. "You" must have done something. How do "you" close the perceived distance between yourself and God? The message remains silent on this. "You" must determine what you did to make God seem distant. "You" must decide how to resolve the problem. And "you" must reestablish your close relationship with God.

This kind of story only raises other questions. Does God move? We do not know. More importantly, *is* he moved? Does he care about me? Again, we lack an answer. In a story where God is apparently both unmoving and unmoved, and in which all the problems revert to me, the world begins to grow dark very quickly.

Psalm 13 and the Story in the Lament

In contrast to the billboard's cynicism, the Psalms shine like the noonday sun. Together, they tell a far more satisfying story of redemption. From a vantage point of grief, the laments call out to the LORD, "Rescue me!" From the opposite side, the psalms of praise answer, "Praise God, he saved me! Let me tell you how." In other words, resolution in the Psalms is more than a theory. It is real.

Psalm 13 is a lament of David, stripped to its barest essentials. It contains characters in conflict, it presents both the means to resolve the dispute, and it features a resolution. Since the Psalm is short, we will show the entire text here.

> How long, O LORD? Will you forget me forever?
> How long will you hide your face from me?
> How long must I take counsel in my soul
>   and have sorrow in my heart all the day?
> How long shall my enemy be exalted over me?
>
> Consider and answer me, O LORD my God;
>   light up my eyes, lest I sleep the sleep of death,
> lest my enemy say, "I have prevailed over him,"
>   lest my foes rejoice because I am shaken.
>
> But I have trusted in your steadfast love;
>   my heart shall rejoice in your salvation.
> I will sing to the LORD,
>   because he has dealt bountifully with me.
>
> —Psalm 13

Even a cursory reading of this psalm shows a dynamic relationship with God. David has a voice. When God is distant, David cries, "How long...?" He calls to God to be moved by his plight and to resolve the conflict between himself and his enemy. And he closes with a sudden realization that God is going to act on his behalf.

A closer look will show us how the three story elements—conflict, escalation, and resolution—develop in this psalm.

Part I: David's Address and Lament, (Verses 1-2)

Unlike the billboard, which features only two characters, this lament has three. The third character makes all the difference in the way we can approach the dilemma. Here are the characters in the order in which they occur in the psalm:

- The LORD: David's opening words are urgent. "How long, O LORD...?" The call, "How long," occurs four times in the first two verses. Its urgency is far more radical than what the billboard theology ever would allow. David's relationship with his God is dynamic. God does not just "seem" distant. He is absent, and David feels the full right to cry out over his situation—even if it means yelling at the top of his lungs. We never read, "Oh, God seems distant. I must have messed something up."
- David, as "I": The second character is David, the one doing the talking. Unlike the "you" on the billboard, David has a voice, and he uses it. "Will you forget me forever? / How long will you hide your face from me?" (verse 1). He challenges God to reveal himself. His third call to the LORD unleashes the complaint: "How long must I take counsel in my soul / and have sorrow in my heart all the day?" (verse 2, beginning). Again, this is radically different from the billboard thinking. The grace that allows David to praise God for his acts of deliverance also allows him to complain in his absence. Sorrow has eclipsed praise, and that fact alone calls for David to cry out to God to do something about the situation.
- A third character, missing entirely from the billboard theology, is an enemy who blasphemes. "How long shall my enemy be exalted over me?" (verse 2, ending). The enemy's identity and actions remain unstated. All we know is that he is delighted by David's misfortune. We cannot emphasize the enemy's importance in the laments too strongly. An enemy of some sort appears in almost every personal psalm of lament. Westermann writes, "One of the acts of the enemy is what they say....The enemy mocks the lamenter, rejoices at his stumbling and falling, revels in his or her misfortune....Almost all these statements are characterized by two interrelated concerns: (1) The speech of the enemy seeks the destruction of the lamenter. (2) The enemy's actual intention is hidden behind lies and false accusations."[28]

The almost universal presence of the three characters maintains the dynamic in lament theology. This element is what makes this psalm and others like it so genuine.

We must recognize a second distinction between the billboard theology and the theology of lament. David's "I" replaces the message's understood, "you." The psalmists never point an accusing finger with the words, "Guess who moved?" Rather than talking *at* an implied audience, the poetry in the laments reflects the writers' genuine struggle with their faith. Their immersion in grief invites us to connect with them. Through their complaints, they articulate our difficulties. God's relationship with David is far deeper than that of a tyrant standing with his arms crossed and saying, "Hey, you moved again." He creates a relationship filled with meaning.

David's Petition to God, (verses 3-4)

The second stanza contains David's prayer to God, with a comment on the consequences if God fails to answer. The prayer takes place in the first two lines: "Consider and answer me, O LORD my God; / light up my eyes..." (Ps. 13:3). I love the metaphor, "Light up my eyes." Its meaning spans the centuries. Bright eyes always signify vitality. We use the picture when we describe our pets. When a dog or a cat has gotten over a period of sickness or other lethargy and has become more responsive to us, we notice, "Her eyes are brighter." David has this picture in mind. "Restore my vitality."

If God fails to fulfill David's request, the consequences will be dire:

> Consider and answer me, O LORD my God;
>> light up my eyes, lest I sleep the sleep of death.
> lest my enemy say, "I have prevailed over him,"
>> lest my foes rejoice because I am shaken.

> —Psalm 13:3-4

The conditional statements are real. David's enemy snaps at his heels, eager to destroy him. The consequences, should such an event occur, represent far more than personal defeat. God will have let his man down, the enemy will continue to blaspheme, and God's foes will think they have won a victory over God. David's defeat will bring shame to God.

The biblical writers in both the Old and New Testaments understand that God's relationship with his people carries two-way significance. If relationships are to be meaningful, they must accept shared responsibility. Therefore, when God's people suffer, God suffers. Unlike the unmoved and unmoving God of the billboard, the biblical God cares for his people every moment of every day. He wants them to cry out to him when they suffer. This relationship forms the basis for one of Jesus' last teachings before his death. Here is what he says in Matthew about the final judgment and God's reception of those who showed mercy to his people:

> Then the King will say to those on his right, "Come, you who are blessed by my Father, inherit the kingdom prepared for you from the foundation of the world. For I was hungry and you gave me food, I was thirsty and you gave me drink, I was a stranger and you welcomed me, I was naked and you clothed me, I was sick and you visited me, I was in prison and you came to me." Then the righteous will answer him, saying, "Lord when did we see you hungry and feed you, or thirsty and give you drink? And when did we see you a stranger and welcome you, or naked and clothe you? And when did we see you sick or in prison and visit you?" And the King will answer them, "Truly, I say to you, *as you did it to one of the least of these my brothers, you did it to me.*"
>
> —Matthew 25:34-40, emphasis added

Unlike the silent and unmovable divine character on the billboard, the biblical God cares so deeply for his people that he cannot help but reply to the suffering in the world. To state the matter in practical terms, David knows that his cry, "How long, O LORD," will have an answer, because he knows that his God cares.

David's Confession of Trust and Vow of Praise, (verses 5-6)

The last stanza depicts an abrupt and absolute change of mood. After his petition against his enemy, David bursts into a song of praise.

> But I have trusted in your steadfast love;
> my heart shall rejoice in your salvation."

—Psalm 13:5

The abrupt appearance of optimism is neither an emotional sleight of hand nor the song of a super-spiritual Christian who has developed the ability to compartmentalize his problems and then ignore them. David's words reveal a genuine understanding that God has his back. Modern translations cannot portray the force in the original language.

The critical clause is the opening, "But I have trusted..." The Hebrew language lacks a word for "but." Instead, it uses the word, "and," which is formed by adding a single letter, *vav,* as a suffix to a noun. The letter *vav* looks like an upended hockey stick pointing to the left. In this case, the text combines the *vav* suffix to an added pronoun, "I," to form the compound word, "And-I." Obviously, the meaning is "But-I." Biblical scholars call this structure a *vav*-adversative to signify the change in mood.[29] When placed against the already complete verb, "I-have-trusted," the literal reading becomes, "But I—I have trusted..." David's confidence in his God is evident.

In this case, the *vav*-adversative signifies an epiphany. David knows that God will rescue him. God has answered his prayer before any action takes place. This occurrence demonstrates the dynamic relationship between the worshiper and God in the Bible.

> During the praying of these Psalms no miracle has occurred, but something else has occurred. God has heard and inclined himself to the one praying; God has had mercy on him....And in this the decisive event has taken place. That which is yet to come, the turning point in the situation, must of necessity follow. Therefore it can now already be regarded as realized.[30]

Having received a spiritual confirmation that God will work on his behalf, David concludes the psalm with a triumphal note:

> I will sing to the LORD,
> because he has dealt bountifully with me.

—Psalm 13:6

This section marks one of the most important components of the laments, the vow of praise. While an explicit promise may be absent, the vow remains an integral part of the lament. The vow is just what it sounds like—a promise to perform a public retelling of what God has done. All biblical praise is public. "In the vow he promises to praise God, to make his name great....The vow of praise therefore means in simple words that he will tell others what God has done for him."[31]

The vow of praise bridges the chasm between lament and praise. It is the crucial element that recognizes that God's relationship with his people is never static. It is genuine, active, and concrete.

Conclusion

Have you ever noticed how pain or loss creates a great depth of character in some people while it leaves others in bitterness? I believe this is partly due to our expectations during our periods of suffering. Regarding those who grow, C.S. Lewis writes,

> We are, not metaphorically but in very truth, a Divine work of art, something that God is making, and therefore something with which He will not be satisfied until it has a certain character.[32]

The character that Lewis describes cannot rise to the surface without pain. Pain itself is incapable of producing character, but God's grace can work through the agency of grief. The Apostle Paul expresses this truth in a marvelous passage from the book of Romans:

> Therefore, since we have been justified by faith, we have peace with God through our Lord Jesus Christ. Through him we have also obtained access by faith into this grace in which we stand, and we rejoice in hope of the glory of God. More than that, we rejoice in our sufferings, knowing that suffering produces endurance, and endurance produces character, and character produces hope, and hope does not put us to shame, because God's love has been poured into our hearts through the Holy Spirit who has been given to us.

> —Romans 5:1-5

Anyone who possesses admirable character—the kind to which others gravitate when they suffer—learns it through suffering. Long-term suffering produces endurance. When patience begins to impress itself into the fiber of a person's being, so that he or she begins to step into a rhythm of maintaining a principled walk, we call that character.

This truth raises a difficulty, however. When Paul says, "We rejoice in our sufferings," his statement appears to contradict everything that David says in Psalm 13. The situation almost has the tension of a boxing match. In the one corner, David, in the dark trunks, cries out, "How long, O LORD?" In the other, Paul wears white trunks, tells us to rejoice. On the surface, one will have to go down for the ten-count.

Is the situation that simple? Is Paul trying to tell us to laugh at pain because we have a guaranteed future in glory? Is he talking about a spiritual Pollyanna experience when a person remains forever optimistic and immune to pain?

Of course not. Paul sought deliverance from suffering. In 2 Corinthians 12, he relates what he calls a personal thorn in the flesh that he was forced to endure. In describing the difficulty, Paul writes, "Three times I pleaded with the Lord about this, that it should leave me" (2 Corinthians 12:8). Ultimately he had to accept that his suffering would remain with him. His personal resolution in 2 Corinthians becomes his operating "Therefore I will boast all the more gladly of my weaknesses, so that the power of Christ may rest upon me. For the sake of Christ, then, I am content with weaknesses, insults, hardships, persecutions, and calamities. For when I am weak, then I am strong" (2 Corinthians 12:9b-10). The power of Christ lays the groundwork for pain and grace in Romans.

The Romans passage remembers the bridge from lament to praise. Paul knows that God hears his children's pleas, and this gives him the freedom to confront the Lord. But he also knows that God uses suffering to complete his work of art. Suffering produces endurance, which builds character. Character in turn produces the ability to see beyond the immediate circumstances to a hopeful future.

Compare Paul's teaching to David's words. What does David do in his psalm? In his lament he begins to show a level of character that can mature only through adversity. In the end—abruptly—he grasps the hope that hope protect him from shame. To borrow from Paul's line of reasoning, David's transformation comes about because God's love has been poured into his heart through the Holy Spirit. David's resolution in Psalm 13:5-6 says in effect, "I know with certainty that God will bring me through this difficulty. Therefore I praise him in my sufferings for the work he is going to do." Lament is *not* a determination to endure our pain with gritted teeth. It is a cry for God to show us his Holy Spirit poured into our hearts. Nor is lament a manipulative tool for us to use to escape suffering. Sometimes God removes our difficulty, while at other times he chooses to take us through it. Either way, our cry to God for deliverance is an act of worship.

Journal Entry

From the one pole, lament calls out to God to rescue us from our adversaries, and vows to praise the Lord publically when he answers. From the other, the praises in the Psalms are testimonies of God's actions on our behalf. They are never just repetitious happy words. They proclaim, "This is how I felt when I was in distress, and this is how God answered me. Come and praise the Lord with me."

What is your "How long, O LORD?" cry? _____

_____

_____

_____

Who or what is your enemy, and how does the enemy threaten your relationship with God? _____

_____

_____

How do you plan to bring praise to God when he delivers you from your pain? _____

_____

_____

CHAPTER 6

Psalm 9/10
Hunger for Justice

You never know how much you really believe anything until its truth or falsehood becomes a matter of life and death to you.[33]

Justice.

It is not a subject we think about often. Unless someone is a philosophy geek, we are unlikely to hear a dinner conversation like this:

> "How was your day, Honey?"
> "Pretty good. I had some free time, so I thought I'd sit down and think about justice for a while."

Typical conversations deal with ordinary events. "Hi, Honey. What's for dinner?" Or, "You'd better sit down. Dave brought home his report card today." Or, "Sweetheart, remember how you said you'd make an appointment to get the cat spayed?"

Then, one day we find ourselves staring injustice in the face, and the issue eclipses everything else.

- A coworker steals the credit for the work you have done, and you find yourself dismissed from your company.
- A trusted friend or family member betrays you when you are most vulnerable.
- Someone robs you of your possessions, money, or worse.

I had a work friend whose thirty-three-year-old daughter was murdered in North Carolina in 2012. After a multistate manhunt, authorities found and arrested the young woman's boyfriend. He awaited trial in a North Carolina jail for a year and a half before he changed his plea to guilty. During that time, the family suffered unbearable anguish. The community responded with remarkable compassion, and "Justice for Lynne" T-shirts were familiar sights in our town during that time. When we plead for justice, our plea comes from our gut. But what exactly are we asking?

The question is harder than it appears at first. The way we answer it depends on the way we begin to talk about it.

What Is Justice?

We live in a generation that has a radically different conception of justice than what even a generation prior had. My father fought in the European Theater in World War II and defended the notion of justice that I came to take for granted. To deprive anyone of basic human rights because of ethnic background is wrong. No one who witnessed the atrocities in the Nazi death camps asked whether they had the right to force their moral opinions on the butchers who had taken so many lives.

The generation currently going to college cannot defend that premise. When a professor friend taught college ethics on the campus where I worked, he would begin his introductory classes with the question, "Was the Holocaust wrong?"

He told me his students could not give him a definite answer. They had become so saturated in ethical tolerance that they had lost the ability to make absolute moral statements. Instead, they said things like, "What they did was wrong from our point of view, but the people involved in it had a different concept of right and wrong. What right do we have to judge their beliefs by our standards?"

The professor had a practical—and jarring—response. He told them, "Then you won't be able to say anything if I give you all failing grades."

The class erupted. "You can't do that!"

"Why not? If I am not allowed to impose my principles on you, then you cannot dictate what is right or wrong to me."

"But it's not fair."

"You mean it's not *just*."

At that point, the students started to get the picture. If they wanted to operate with a consistent definition of morality in the world, even regarding something as simple as college grades, they needed an unbending standard. For about four or five weeks, my friend would be able to communicate to the class. About midway through the semester, however, the students would revert to the tolerance that they had learned in school

When Justice is a Matter of Life and Death

We need justice. More specifically, we need to know that a once-for-all code of justice exists. The employee who loses his job wrongfully needs it. The betrayed family member needs it. "Justice for Lynne" needs it. Why, then, when we feel the need so strongly, is the concept so difficult?

I believe two reasons exist. One reason, to borrow from the C.S. Lewis quote at the beginning of this chapter, is because justice is less than a matter of life or death under ordinary circumstances. Unless we serve in the military, law enforcement, the legal system, or some other place where we face justice issues routinely, our day-to-day activity keeps us out of contact with the matter of justice. It is not a question that demands our everyday attention.

The deeper reason lies in the way we think. Most people carry an incomplete understanding of what justice is in the first place. We believe that we know our position when in fact we are adrift at sea. People presume justice must be something that looks like tolerance, egalitarianism, moral relativism, or any of the other let's-just-all-get-along manners of thinking. This absence of understanding plagues even those who defend justice. In the summer of 2016, a gunman murdered forty-nine people in a nightclub in Orlando. A couple of days later, Attorney General Loretta Lynch said this at a news conference. "This Department of Justice and your country stands [sic] with you in the light. We stand with you to say that the good in this world far outweighs the evil, that our common humanity transcends our differences, and that our most effective response to terror and to hatred is compassion. It's unity, and it's love."[34]

Excuse me? Justice has nothing to do with the relative weight of good over evil. It has to do with punishing crime and righting wrongs. Justice is more than a vague declaration about balancing enough compassionate acts against a heinous act so we can declare the books to be closed.

The Myth of Moral Neutrality

Defining justice with terms like tolerance, egalitarianism, moral relativism, and compassion assumes the existence of morally neutral territory. If we can exercise enough compassion, unity, and love, as Attorney General Lynch declared, we can neutralize the injustice and everyone will be happy. Neutrality works by a balance of good versus evil, or by consensus. Just find the middle ground, and we can declare the case closed.

In actuality, the quest for neutrality stands on moral bullying. The moment Tom tells Sue, "You can't force your moral views on me," he forces his moral views on Sue. For her to adopt the declared "neutral" ground, she must sacrifice what she holds sacred. Our culture practically worships neutrality, but neutrality is impossible. Somebody's views always come out on top.

The ultimate cause for the confusion is deeper than social inequality, or inadequate education, or immature religious presumptions. These factors may play into the misconception, but the fault ultimately traces back to the early history of Western philosophy.

Socrates, the Man Who Started it All

Some of the earliest and most clearly defined discussions on justice come from the Greek philosopher, Plato, who spanned the fifth and fourth centuries BC. A large body of his work follows the dialogues of his mentor, Socrates. Since Socrates did not write, most of what we know about him comes from Plato's dialogues that feature him Socrates' discussions with others on philosophical issues. Euthyphro (pronounced **You**-thih-fro) is one of the last Socratic dialogues. Briefly, the dialogue is a discussion on doing what is right. More specifically, it is about the fundamental *meaning* of "doing what is right." In Socrates' words, "[W]hat is the essential form of holiness which makes all holy actions holy[?]"[35] The question sounds absurdly easy but turns out to be almost impossibly difficult.

Euthyphro and the Idea of Right

To understand this question fully, we need to go back to the beginning of the dialogue, where Euthyphro meets Socrates on the way to court. Socrates has received a court summons for an issue that ultimately will result in his death sentence, but when he learns about Euthyphro's purpose for going to court, he shifts the focus to the other man. Euthyphro has come to court to bring a murder charge against his father.

Euthyphro is an extraordinary man. He is a man of means, but also one who has refused to let his wealth corrupt his moral beliefs. He is confident about his convictions. The background is simple enough. Euthyphro's father owned a servant who murdered another slave. Because of the crime, the father bound the guilty servant and threw him in a ditch to die of exposure. In other words, the man assumed the roles of judge, jury, and executioner over his slave. Slaves were considered to be the property of their owners, so this was an accepted practice in this time.

This act enrages Euthyphro. In his mind, even though the servant himself is guilty of murder, Euthyphro's father lacks any right to exercise vigilante justice. Therefore, Euthyphro decides that his father will have to pay. An excerpt from the early part of the dialogue will show how confident Euthyphro is.

> EUTHYPHRO: They say that for a son to prosecute his father as a murderer is unjust. How little they know about divinity in its relation to what is just or unjust, Socrates!

> SOCRATES: But by heaven Euthyphro! Do you think you have such an accurate knowledge of things divine, and what is just and unjust, that, in the circumstances you describe, you can accuse your father? Are you not afraid that you yourself might be doing an unholy deed?

> EUTHYPHRO: Socrates, if I did not have an accurate knowledge of matters like that, I would be good for nothing. I would be no different from ordinary men.[36]

Euthyphro exudes confidence. He is a man who is certain about what is right. When Socrates asks him to define the difference between good and evil, Euthyphro jumps in with a ready answer.

> Well, then, I say that justice is what I am doing now—prosecuting the wrongdoer who commits a murder, or a robbery, or any other crimes like those, whether they be someone's father, mother, or anyone else.[37]

Euthyphro's logical direction, though unspoken, is significant. It rests on his personal approach to justice. He has not been content to think about the nature of justice abstractly. In his mind, he has elevated the definition of right by taking it to a higher level than any other civilized human being. He has become the ultimately just man. By his self-proclamation, he assumes the right to take his father to court on a murder charge.

While his words sound noble, Euthyphro has stepped into a minefield without knowing it. Two possible meanings exist for Euthyphro's pronouncement. The more radical possibility is that he is trying to make a new declaration about what is right. If this is the case, he has stepped into the place of God.

Socrates gives him the benefit of the doubt, however, and assumes the less radical possibility. Rather than defining justice, Euthyphro simply has demonstrated a higher example of just actions. For Socrates, an example fails to qualify as a definition, so he asks again, what *is* justice?

The question causes Euthyphro to realize how complicated the issue is, and he has to scramble. His second attempt shifts the focus from himself to the deities. Justice must be what the gods love.

Euthyphro has taken a step in the right direction. At least he has taken himself out of the middle of the definition. Only one point gets in the way. Conflict and treachery drive the gods in Greek mythology. With all that disagreement in the spiritual realms, which god is right about right? Euthyphro finds himself caught in the same dilemma as the college students who have grown up with tolerance teaching. Are certain actions just even when people—or gods—disagree?

After some wrangling, the two men come to a compromise. Justice must be what all the gods all love unanimously. Euthyphro is happy. He has proven his point to the master. Though he has had to step down from his self-proclaimed place on center stage, the new definition acknowledges a base of authority higher than human opinion. If the gods all agree on something, it must be right.

Then, Socrates drops the bomb. He says, "Regarding what is just, is it just because the gods approve it, or do they approve it because it is just?"[38]

In other words, where ultimately does justice originate? What is the quality that makes justice *just*? What is its essence? Do the gods call justice into being by simple consensus, or is it something that stands outside the gods so that even they must conform to it?

If the former alternative is the case, we need to know what makes the gods' opinion so unique that their agreement creates rightness. If justice means only what all the gods agree on, then it becomes nothing more than tolerance lifted from the human level to the divine. What happens when the gods change their minds? After all, this was the argument that my college professor friend's class assumed. We cannot condemn the Nazi extermination of six million Jews, because—like the gods—they colluded. Even if they practiced hatred, their actions right in their collective mind, so we must count it as right.

The gods are in the same position as the mortals. Consensus—even in the divine world—is unable to create justice. Therefore, since the gods must answer to a higher standard, then the ultimate question remains the same. Who defines the standard?

Euthyphro realizes he is no closer to an answer than anyone else. Socrates and Euthyphro have failed to come to a consensus about *what* is right, and now Euthyphro realizes he has yet to find sufficient basis to argue *why* right actions are right. In the end, the essential question remains unresolved.

The matter is critical. In exposing Euthyphro's dilemma, Socrates raised an ethical issue that has remained unanswered in the history of Western philosophy.

Psalm 9/10 and Justice

Enter the pair, Psalms 9 and 10. The thematic material and construction of these two psalms indicate that the two originally may have been a single psalm.[39] In treating them as a unit, I have adopted the title, Psalm 9/10. This psalm of David is both a lament against the injustice from an enemy and cry for the LORD to make the situation right. Three facts will be critical for us as we look at this Psalm.

- One, even though the psalm predates Socrates by several hundred years, David raises the same issues about justice that occur in the Euthyphro dialogue. Therefore, Socrates' questions will be fair game for us to ask in this context.
- Two, God has a great deal to say about justice, and he said it long before Socrates and Euthyphro.
- Three, I will argue that the psalm gives us the answers that eluded Euthyphro and Socrates in their dialogue.

Instead of pressing through the psalm chronologically, we will consider it thematically.

David's Dire Situation

David trouble remains under the surface at first, because he begins with words of praise. His plea will rise out of these words later.

> I will give thanks to the LORD with my whole heart;
> I will recount all of your wonderful deeds.
> I will be glad and exult in you;
> I will sing praise to your name, O Most High.

> —Psalm 9:1-2

These lines form double duty. First, they offer praise to the LORD. Second, they anticipate David's plea for God to intervene in a praiseworthy manner. David will use them as leverage for his cause. They are not manipulative, however. David does not mean to force God's hand into acting. Look closely at the way they begin:

- "I will give thanks..."
- "I will recount..."
- "I will be glad..."
- "I will sing..."

The words here constitute David's vow of praise, the promise that those who mourn now will give praise to God when he intervenes. Therefore, they are spoken more out of faith in what God will do than as a manipulative tool. David knows that God must answer, and when he does, he will be ready to offer praise.

His current situation is dire, and it involves immediate danger from enemies who want him dead.

> Be gracious to me, O LORD!
> See my affliction from those who hate me,
> O you who lift me up from the gates of death.

> —Psalm 9:13

Later in the psalm, David describes the enemy's actions more fully. They are sinister.

> He sits in ambush in the villages;
>   in hiding places he murders the innocent.
> His eyes stealthily watch for the helpless;
>   he lurks in ambush like a lion in his thicket;
> he lurks that he may seize the poor;
>   he seizes the poor when he draws him into his net.
> The helpless are crushed, sink down,
>   and fall by his might.
>
> —Psalm 10:8-10

David's Answer to Euthyphro's First Dilemma: Submission to God's Justice

In Psalm 9:3, we see the first of three crucial differences between David and Euthyphro's conceptions of justice. The first involves David's cause.

> When my enemies turn back,
>   they stumble and perish before your presence.
> For you have maintained my just cause;
>   you have sat on the throne, giving righteous judgment.
>
> —Psalm 9:3-4

"*My* enemies....*my* just cause"? At first glance, David's speech appears to be little better than Euthyphro, who claims to have "an accurate knowledge of matters" regarding justice. When we look at David's words closely, however, we see a much deeper well from which he draws. His enemies will stumble and perish "before *your* presence. / For *you* have maintained my just cause; / *you* have sat on the throne..."

Unlike Euthyphro, David never claims to own justice. He never presumes to be able to walk up to the throne and declare proclamations. When he speaks about his "just cause," he understands himself to be subject to his God at every point.

David's Answer to Euthyphro's Second Dilemma: God's Solemn Commitment to Justice

A major hurdle to finding a functional description of justice in Euthyphro lies in the Greek gods themselves. The ancient Greeks' understanding of the gods came from their mythology, but frankly, the accounts of the Greek gods read like soap operas. They give the people little help in the way of principle.

Euthyphro's attempt to define justice by what the gods believe fails because of the gods' infighting. In a pantheon in which no one can agree, the gods' opinions will be just that—opinions. They are as relativistic in their declaration as Euthyphro was in his original position. They will be "right" only in their own minds.

This tension is absent from the Hebrew mindset. In Psalm 9/10, "right" originates in God's being. He is majestic, and he is free from self-conflict.

> But the LORD sits enthroned forever;
>   he has established his throne for justice.
> and he judges the world with righteousness;
>   he judges the peoples with uprightness.

—Psalm 9:7-8

The God of the Bible is never frivolous. As we saw from the discussion on Job, God knows what his job is, and he is single-minded in his approach to it. The Psalms pick up here. Where Job discusses justice as theory, the Psalms tackle the issue in practical terms. The description in Psalm 9/10 presents a level of purpose and self-awareness lacking in Greek mythology. Human history matters to God, and he has chosen to bring justice to the world. When we cry out for justice, this is the God we want on our side. Here are some of the points that arise from the two verses quoted above:

- Justice originates with God. He has established his throne to administrate justice in the world.
- His judgments go out, according to the psalm, with "righteousness" and "uprightness."
- They are absolute. The descriptive phrase, "enthroned forever," illustrates permanence. God will not allow his standards to change at some later date under someone else's ethical interpretation.

- He rules without apology.
- Nobody assists God in discovering previously untested standards for justice. Since God has spoken authoritatively on justice, neither Euthyphro nor anyone else can set a new yet-unreached bar.

David's Answer to Euthyphro's Third Dilemma: God's Transcendence and Immanence

Euthyphro's amended attempt to arrive at a satisfactory definition of justice—those things that all the gods love unanimously—suffers from wishful thinking. Seriously, can he find even one thing about which they all agree? How many times has the U.S. Congress found anything that all its members love unanimously?

Socrates concedes this point, however, because he wants to raise the third and most severe question. Does the gods' love for something *make* that something just, or do the gods love it *because* it is just?

No matter where we begin the dialogue, this is the final question on the origin of justice. Where does it come from, and to whom does it belong?

David's answer is the same for both questions. Justice comes from God alone, and it belongs to God alone. This is the basis for his declaration of God as judge, quoted above. To understand this principle, we must come back to the doctrine of transcendence and discuss the balancing doctrine of immanence in more detail.

Transcendence: When David writes, But the LORD sits enthroned forever; / he has established his throne for justice (Psalm 9:7), he refers to God's transcendence. Transcendence refers to God's separateness from his creation. He is fundamentally different from anything else in the cosmos. For example,

- God alone is eternal. The creation came into being because he brought it into being. "In the beginning, God created the heavens and the earth" (Genesis 1:1).
- God alone is self-existent. Everything else exists because he has made it. One of the creation Psalms reads, "Of old you laid the foundation of the earth, / and the heavens are the work of your hands. / They will perish, but you will remain..." (Psalm 102:25-26).
- God holds sovereign rights over his creation, including his right to establish his throne to judge his creatures.

We call the totality of these qualities transcendence. Think about Socrates' question about the origin of justice. Does God act because the action is just, or does the work become just because God does it? The answer is neither. David's declaration, "He has established His throne for judgment," answers the question.

- God's actions do not reflect his principles. They reflect his character. When he rules, he reveals his personal cause.
- God's self-direction is the most important point to understand about the origin of justice. *His judgments are just because they are his. His judgments are eternal and unchangeable.*

Immanence: In our minds, God's declaration of sovereign rights raises an immediate red flag. If God works alone, then how do we know whether his actions are right? How do we know justice is good? How do we know *he* is good?

The doctrine of immanence helps answer those questions. Immanence means that God is near. And by "near" we mean both that he is both approachable and inescapable. Psalm 139 is a meditation on God's nearness. Part of the psalm reads,

> Where shall I go from your Spirit?
> Or where shall I flee from your presence?
> If I ascend to heaven, you are there!
> If I make my bed in Sheol [the grave], you are there!
> If I take the wings of the morning
> and dwell in the uttermost parts of the sea,
> even there your hand shall lead me,
> and your right hand shall hold me...
>
> —Psalm 139:7-10

In the context of Psalm 9/10, immanence means that God cares for us. It means that though he declares justice, he also describes it in terms that are intensely meaningful to those for whom justice is a matter of life and death. Look at the rich terminology that the psalm uses to illustrate God's immanence:

> The LORD is *a stronghold for the oppressed,*
> a stronghold in times of trouble.
> And those who know your name *put their trust in you,*
> for you, O LORD, *have not forsaken those who*
> *seek you....*
>
> For he who avenges blood *is mindful of them;*
> he *does not forget the cry of the afflicted....*
>
> The LORD has *made himself known;* he has *executed*
> *judgment;*
> the wicked are snared in the work of their own hands.
>
> —Psalm 9:9/10, 12, 16, emphasis added

For those who wait for justice, at least five points rise from these verses.

- God's justice differentiates between good and evil. He cares for the oppressed.
- His justice illustrates his trustworthiness. He does not forsake those who seek him.
- His justice is genuine. He avenges blood on behalf of the afflicted.
- His justice is approachable. He makes himself known to the humble as the ultimately just God.
- His justice is just. The wicked find themselves snared by their deeds, either logically or by consequence.

Waiting for Justice

Everyone struggles with these concepts. I first engaged them in my freshman year at college, when we studied Euthyphro in an introductory ethics course. I mulled over the issue for the next five years before the moment came when I understood the interrelation between God's transcendence and immanence.

Of course, few of us possess that philosophical bent. But for those who wait for justice, the issue matters more than food or sleep. Its absence saps their souls. I wrote earlier about a murder involving a friend's daughter. A year and a half after the incident, I caught up with my friend. Her grief was still raw. When we talked, she asked me, "Why does it have to hurt so much?"

The answer that came to mind was, "Because we love so much," but I knew that it was neither what she wanted or needed. She needed someone to listen. Similarly, answering the question is only the secondary point of this chapter. The primary point is to let you know that God cares about justice when it concerns you. Therefore, I want to conclude with some thoughts that speak to those who live in a justice vacuum. What does justice mean for the oppressed?

More than anything else, this psalm allows us to fight for justice in this life. We know this: even if justice fails to come by the hands of the men and women whose job it is to serve it, it will come at God's hand, and when it does, it will be unstoppable. Continue to cry out. Your voice tells the world that you will settle for nothing less than hope. Hope is both a powerful and terrifying virtue, especially for those who minister. "Bringing hurt to public expression is an important first step in the dismantling criticism that permits a new reality, theological and social, to emerge."[40]

The closing of the psalm can be your prayer.

> Arise, O LORD; O God, lift up your hand;
>   forget not the afflicted.
> Why does the wicked renounce God
>   and say in his heart, "You will not call to account?"
> But you do see, for you note mischief and vexation,
>   that you may take it into your hands;
> to you the helpless commits himself:
>   you have been the helper of the fatherless.
> Break the arm of the wicked and evildoer;
>   call his wickedness to account till you find none.
>
> The LORD is king forever and ever;
>   the nations perish from his land.
> O LORD, you hear the desire of the afflicted;
>   you will strengthen their heart; you will incline
>   your ear
> to do justice to the fatherless and the oppressed,
>   so that man who is of the earth may strike terror no
>   more.
>
> —Psalm 10:12-18

One Bible commentator writes this comment on the psalm.

> God does not postpone judgment and salvation *until the end of the world*, although times of trouble come for the pious and days of apparent victory for their enemies. He already judges *in history* individuals and nations, so that all traces of them are *blotted out* from the earth, and their name is *forgotten*. He likewise saves, blesses and raises up others who take *refuge* with Him and put the *trust* in Him.[41]

Psalm 9/10 is not a plea for ultimate justice at the end of time, but for judgment right now. The active presence of justice marks its greatest hope.

Journal Entry

What is my cause, and how does God help me maintain it (Psalm 9:4)? _____

_____

_____

_____

What have my enemies done to me, and why are their actions unjust (Psalm 10:7-11)? _____

_____

_____

_____

As we have seen, the LORD gives us a wide latitude in calling for justice against the oppressors (Psalm 10:12-15). At the same time, he tests everyone's motivations, regardless of whether we are among the oppressors or the oppressed (Psalm 9:7-8). What guidelines have I erected for myself to keep my prayer for justice from crossing the border and becoming a prayer for personal vengeance? _____

_____

_____

_____

A plea for the LORD to perform justice is more than a rant. It is a prayer that is rooted both in trust and in the reality of the present situation. (Psalm 9:17-20). How do I plan to demonstrate my belief that he will act for me? _____

_____

_____

_____

CHAPTER 7

Psalm 77
Finding God in the Dark

Love God? Sometimes I hate him.
—Martin Luther[42]

The *Love Story* Mentality

For those old enough to remember the cultural revolution during the 1960s and early '70s, the romantic tragedy, *Love Story,* stands as one of its monuments. The movie's famous line, "Love means never having to say you're sorry," became a cultural icon. During the love generation, the saying was a romanticist's rallying cry. Of course, it was only the grown up version of "happily ever after." Each involves wistful thinking. Real love means being able to say we are sorry, and then enjoying forgiveness and reconciliation.

In this chapter, I want to look at a similar assumption regarding Christian maturity. "Proper" protocol lays down an unwritten rule that says, "Faith means never having to tell God you're dissatisfied." The practice requires us to make three moral assumptions:

- One, we may express our faith only in positive terms.
- Two, we must believe at all times.
- Three, we are never allowed to express doubt.

Here is the truth, however. Everyone's faith falters, we all stumble in our belief, and we all succumb to doubt more often than we would care to admit. In fact, if we were honest, we would have to confess that sometimes we become downright angry at God.

When life begins to look futile, we have three logical choices. One, we can become cynical and fold into ourselves. The term *cynical* goes beyond cynical humor. I mean the deeper, what's-the-use kind of cynicism that questions our most fundamental beliefs. The cynicism of this sort accomplishes nothing but taking us one step closer to abandoning hope altogether.

Two, we can slip into the *Love Story* mentality and pretend everything is all right. To convince everyone—especially ourselves—that we are spiritually mature, we deny that we have a problem with God. Our choice may uphold the three unwritten moral assumptions about faith, at least on the surface. But it leaves a gaping hole in one of the written moral assumptions. We lie to ourselves and God.

The third—and I will argue proper—choice is to speak our feelings out loud to God. For those who have grown up in an environment where we are taught to revere God under all circumstances, this choice lies somewhere between painful and unthinkable. We are terrified either by the thought itself, or the consequences, or both. Yet the psalmists expressed these ideas. Out loud.

Psalm 77 and Asaph's Anger toward God

Psalm 77, a psalm of Asaph, is an example of such speech. In fact, the psalm is a confession of Asaph's complete disenchantment with God. He is dried up, fed up, and at a total loss to find even a single positive memory of God's work in his life. When we find ourselves in a spiritual desert, this is refreshing news. Someone has been here before us, and his experience has left its footprint in the Bible. Here are some of the truths the Psalms will teach us:

- Happiness is not a prerequisite for spiritual maturity.
- We do not have to pretend everything is all right when it is not.
- God will not break us when we tell him what is on our minds. Psalm 139:4 says, "Even before a word is on my tongue, / behold, O LORD, you know it altogether." That means he knows our

thoughts before we think them. You will not hear him say, "Well, I'm *incensed*."

- None of the Psalms portrays worship as putting on spiritual airs to impress our friends. They are about honest mourning and praise before God.
- The Psalms give us permission to be dissatisfied and even angry with God.
- They allow us to ask questions out loud.

The Psalm 77 Superscript and the Darker Psalms

The superscript to Psalm 77 reads, "To the choirmaster, according to Jeduthun. A Psalm of Asaph." Asaph and Jeduthun fall among the supporting cast in the sweep of biblical history, rather than the main actors. Outside of a few scattered references, they appear almost exclusively either in the book of Psalms or the Chronicles, the priestly commentary on Israel's history.

Still, their assigned duties in United Israel's worship were important. During the eleventh century BC, Israel's first two kings, Saul and David, spanned the formative years when God's people's identity grew from "the descendants of Israel," a loosely knit ethnic group, to "Israel" as a nation with a particular mode of worship. Both Saul and David were instrumental in contributing to Israel's national identity. David's writings would become a legacy that the later priestly writers of the Chronicles would stress in their history. His dream was to build a temple for the LORD in Jerusalem. Worship coursed through his veins.

Asaph and Jeduthun became partners in ministry with David. According to the Chronicles, the two men shared David's dream to develop a national worship identity. Along with a third musician named Heman, they led the early praises of Israel.

1 Chronicles 16 gives us this summary regarding Asaph, Heman, and Jeduthun during David's reign as king:

> So David left Asaph and his brothers there before the ark
> of the covenant of the LORD to minister regularly before
> the ark as each day required....and he left Zadok the priest
> and his brothers the priests before the tabernacle of the

> LORD in the high place that was at Gibeon....With them
> were Heman and Jeduthun and the rest of those *chosen*
> *and expressly named to give thanks to the LORD, for his*
> *steadfast love endures forever.*
>
> —1 Chronicles 16:37, 39, 41

Asaph wrote many of the hymns that would find their way into the national hymnal. Heman and Jeduthun worked with him as instrumentalists. Each has at least one contribution to the Psalms. Here the emphasized portion of the quote above becomes significant. The three were "expressly named to give thanks to the LORD, for his steadfast love endures forever." If we were to cast this description in a contemporary worship team job description, we would expect this to translate to praise. Instead, all three wrote about dark subjects.

Among the three, Asaph is the hymn writer. Twelve psalms—Psalms 50 and 73-83—bear his name as the author. His works include laments, historical lessons, and essays on wisdom, but they lack a single unadulterated praise psalm. From the content in Asaph's psalms we see the man as a serious, and at times, troubled thinker, yet God chose to include his dark thoughts in the book of Psalms.

Heman's name appears once, over Psalm 88, as the person responsible for its musical notation. This psalm is the darkest personal lament in the book and the only one to end without hope. We will discuss it in the next chapter.

Jeduthun contributed to three psalms, Psalms 39, 62, and 77. Like Heman, he appears to have set up the musical arrangements for them. All three are laments, and in each, the writer finds himself stunned to silence for one reason or another. All three express discontentment with God, but Psalm 77 lays it down like asphalt.

Asaph and Jeduthun's Partnership in Psalm 77

How does a person write a hymn against God? And having written it, whom does he find to set it to music?

Understandably, no one takes this task lightly. Our dark thoughts are our own. We do not open them to just anyone. The person in whom we confide has to be both trustworthy and sympathetic toward us. I cannot be dogmatic about this, but I believe Asaph partnered with Jeduthun on Psalm 77 because Jeduthun was familiar with the kind of grief that plagued his friend. I believe Asaph needed someone who understood his dilemma on the deepest level, and for that reason chose Jeduthun.

As the chapter introducing the Psalms stressed, all worship in Israel falls between the two poles of lament and praise. Neither praise nor lament in the Psalms exists in isolation, and neither ever forgets the other. For this reason, Asaph, Heman, and Jeduthun can offer laments without any sense of contradiction toward their assignment. They understand that lament is a cry to the LORD to deliver. Laments exist as prayers for the LORD to restore the writers' joy. I am confident that when we realize our right to express our honest feelings toward God—even when they are bitter—the journey from mourning to praise for "the LORD, whose steadfast love endures forever" has begun.

Part I: The Day of My Distress (verses 1-3)

Psalm 77 unfolds in seven episodes, symmetrically arranged around its middle section. It commences with a complaint and ends with a hymn of praise. Ultimately the psalm is less about finding resolution than it is demonstrating the resolve to hold on to the truth. This study will follow Bible commentator Samuel Terrien's outline:

> Part I: The Day of My Distress (verses 1-3)
> Part II: My Music Playing (verses 4-6)
> Part III: Has God Rejected His People? (verses 7-9)
> Part IV: I Remember the Deeds of the Lord (verses 10-12)
> Part III': Thou Hast Redeemed (verses 13-15)
> Part II': The Waters Have Seen Thee (verses 16-17)
> Part I': Thou Didst Lead Thy People (verses 18-20)[43]

The opening lines suggest a scene from a film. Picture a man standing in the middle of a torrential rainstorm, with hands extended to heaven. With gritted teeth, he wails,

> I cry aloud to God,
> > aloud to God, and he will hear me.
> In the day of my trouble I seek the Lord;
> > in the night my hand is stretched out without
> > wearying;
> > my soul refuses to be comforted.
> When I remember God, I moan;
> > When I meditate, my spirit faints.

—Psalm 77:1-2

God remains silent, and Asaph remains angry. Psalm 77 aims more *at* God than *to* him. Most laments are dramas involving three characters: the writer; an adversary who is hostile toward the writer; and the LORD, to whom the author presents his case. This psalm has only two characters: Asaph and God. No outside adversary exists because God has become the enemy. Asaph's frustration with God becomes evident when we examine the way he addresses God.

- In verse 1, he uses the Hebrew word *Elohim*, the descriptive word for God.
- Verse 2 contains the term, "the Lord," as a capitalized title, rather than "the LORD" in lower case caps. The two terms are English conventions used to indicate Hebrew titles for God. The English rendering, "The Lord," signifies the Hebrew word, *Adonai*, which means, "My Master." The term, "the LORD," in all caps, refers to the designation, refers to *Yahweh*, or Jehovah, the Old Testament covenant name of God. The name, Yahweh, or its shortened form, Yah, is the covenant name for God. *Yah* appears only once in this psalm.

The name of Yahweh in the laments is critical. Go to almost any lament, and you will find the petitioner crying out to God by name. Here are some samples from the opening Psalms:

- "Yahweh, how many are my foes!...Arise, Yahweh! / Save me, O my God!" (Ps. 3:1, 7).
- "Give ear to my words, Yahweh; / consider my groaning" (Ps. 5:1)

- "Yahweh, rebuke me not in your anger..." (Ps. 6:1a)
- "Why, Yahweh, do you stand afar off? / Why do you hide yourself in times of trouble? (Ps. 10:1).

The reason for the repeated use of God by name is because the psalms of lament are bound up in the writers' covenant relationship with their God, and Yahweh is God's covenant name.

When Asaph writes, "I cry aloud to *God*....In the day of my trouble I seek *my Master*" (Ps. 77:1a, 2a), he sets up an act of distancing that borders on insult. Imagine a drama in which an adolescent has become so angry at his father that he refuses to call him Dad and resorts to his professional title. When the father tries to reach out, the young man says something like, "I'm sorry, Major. I guess I'll never make the cut like you did." Such is Asaph's level of distress. Asaph says, "When I remember God I *moan*; / when I meditate, *my spirit faints*" (verse 3). In simple terms, his words mean, "The thought of God makes me feel sick."

Part II: My Music Playing (verses 4-6)

The street where my wife Patty and I used to live runs along the length of a glacial ridge, about halfway up. At the east end, our street comes to a T-intersection on a one-block street that runs from the top to the bottom of the ridge. Because of the steep grade, the street on the hill is called Race Street. Our street appears to have been added as an afterthought during our city's early development because the space between the two houses allows for only a single lane. The street lies about four feet from the house on the upward side of the hill and fifteen feet from the house on the lower side. Because of the hill, the cut is significant. The street grade runs a couple of inches below the upper house's basement floor, leaving the house's entire basement wall exposed. At some point, the owners cut out a section of the exposed wall, installed a garage door, and poured a concrete ramp. Their basement now doubles as a garage.

Last summer I spoke to a man who repairs and paints rental properties in our area. He told me he had worked in the corner house several times, and finally became curious about a padlocked door on the inside of the basement garage. He broke the lock off and found a stairway going down to a sub-basement level—eighteen stairs that led down to an arched brick

87

room, a basement beneath the first basement. The room probably was a fruit and vegetable cellar in its early years, but it rests two levels underground.

The second basement makes a perfect picture of Asaph's situation. In this psalm, he finds himself stuck in the hidden brick room. His situation suffocates his joy. His encounter with God is bitter. He continues his personal experience with the words,

> You hold my eyelids open;
> I am so troubled that I cannot speak.
>
> —Psalm 77:4

He is both sleepless and speechless. Even the worship alternatives dry up. When he tries to find solace in his past adoration, even his personal history comes up empty.

> I said, "Let me remember my song in the night;
> let me meditate in my heart."
> Then my spirit made a diligent search...
>
> —Psalm 77:5-6

And his diligent search brought him nothing. The entire content of the third section consists of rhetorical—and unanswered—questions.

Part III: Has God Rejected His People? (verses 7-9)

After his search, Asaph finds only frustration.

> Will the Lord spurn forever,
> and never again be favorable?
> Has his steadfast love forever ceased?
> Are his promises [lit. Is his word] at an end for all
> time?
> Has God forgotten to be gracious?
> Has he in anger shut up his compassion?" *Selah*[44]
>
> —Psalm 77:7-9

We tend to keep situations like this to ourselves, partly because we know that others will break out Christian clichés, like, "Be joyful, because the joy of the Lord is your strength." Or, "Set your mind on things above...." Or, "Whatever is true, whatever is honorable, whatever is just, whatever is pure...think about these."

But the sayings remain clichés. For a person like Asaph, who has sought for joy in vain, who has looked for light and found nothing but darkness, and who has tried to meditate on past accomplishments only to find empty cupboards, encouragements like these feel more like cattle prods than salve.

We all have experienced times when life has felt like a spiritual Dust Bowl. The fact that we use terms like "spiritual dryness," and "desert experience" attests to the reality. That leaves us with a question. Why do sincere believers fall into depressive states of mind that make us feel like God has abandoned us?

I will be honest. I lack an answer to that question.

I can tell you this, however. I have been in these valleys more than once, and despite my best efforts to guard against them, I know I will visit them again. They are a fact of life for those who live by faith. That means that the over-the-counter relief pills— "Pick out four verses from the pain-reliever section and swallow them three times a day"—fails to satisfy. It never has and it never will. When our cry becomes, "Will the Lord spurn forever...Has God forgotten to be gracious?" we need more than candy cough drops. We need to reconnect to our faith foundation.

Part IV: I Remember the Deeds of the Lord (verses 10-12)

Asaph realizes this. Verse 10 marks the turning point of the psalm. The English Standard Version reads,

> Then I said, "I will appeal to this,
> *to the years* of the right hand of the Most High."

> —Psalm 77:10 ESV, emphasis added

In the original language, the verse begins with a *vav*-adversative, making the literal meaning, "But I said..." In other words, Asaph is signaling the point where his thinking changes.

After this point, the verse becomes a difficult verse to interpret. The critical word is *shnŏt*. In the form in which it appears in the text, it can be either a noun meaning *years;* or a verb meaning *to change.* The spelling and diacritical markings are identical. The situation is similar to what we encounter with the English word, *bear.* As a noun, it signifies an animal in the woods. As a verb, it means to carry or support. Context determines which use we apply.

In the case of the psalm, the context allows the meaning to make sense in either rendition. For example, the English Standard Version renders the term, "years":

> Then I said, "I will appeal to this,
>   to the *years* of the right hand of the Most High."

> —Psalm 77:10, ESV, emphasis added

The context of verses 11 to the end of the psalm, which appeals to God's ancient wisdom, supports this interpretation. Bible versions such as King James, New King James, and the New International Version have adopted this understanding of the verse.

On the other hand, the New Living Bible, Revised Standard Version, and New American Standard Version have settled on the meaning, "to change," for the disputed word. The emphasis on change draws contextual support from the first nine verses of the psalm. The Revised Standard Version is representative of this family of translations:

> Then I said, "It is my grief that the right hand of the Most High *has changed.*"

> —Psalm 77:10 RSV, emphasis added

I prefer this second option. The focus at this point shifts from an appeal to God to Asap's personal discourse. He has been on a collision course with his thoughts, and in a moment of self-revelation, he sees the need to change his line of thinking.[45] The sentiment describes a universal turning point in the grief experience when sufferers realize the time has come to settle accounts with their emotions. It marks the beginning of acceptance.

Regardless of the wording, the sentiment remains the same. Whether Asaph looks back and tell himself, "This is my grief speaking," or he makes the more forward-looking determination, "I will appeal to the years of the right hand of the Most High," he signifies determination to move on from his grief.

Immediately after this verse, Asaph appeals to *Yahweh,* the covenant name of God, here in the shortened form, *Yah.* His use of the personal name does not signify a reconnection with his God. Instead, it signals a teeth-gritting act of determination to look beyond his emotional crash-and-burn and apply what he knows to be true.

> I will remember the deeds of the LORD [Hebrew, *Yah*];
> yes, I will remember your wonders of old.
> I will ponder all your work,
> and meditate on your mighty deeds.
>
> —Psalm 77:11-12

Look at the "I will" statements in these two verses. The original language contains four affirmations:

I will remember the deeds of the LORD.
I will remember your wonders....
I will ponder....
I will meditate....

Asaph's pairing of the words "remember" and "meditate" in this section is deliberate. Earlier he had written, "When I *remember* God, I moan; / when I *meditate,* my spirit faints" (verse 3), and, "Let me *remember* my song in the night; / let me *meditate* in my heart" (verse 6). The earlier references looked back to his attempt to bring up successes from his personal past devotional life. They have led to frustration. He must dig deeper, and the ground where he chooses to dig contains two great acts of God.

Parts III′, II′, and I′: The Resolve to Praise (verses 13-20)

The answer comes by way of his theology, what he knows to be right about God. For the ancient Hebrews, faith and narrative form complimentary bars of a helix. In this case, the narrative involves two of the greatest events in

Old Testament history: the Exodus from Egypt and the Red Sea crossing. The conclusion reads in part,

> Your way, O God, is holy.
>> What god is great like our God?
> You are the God who works wonders;
>> you have made known your might among the peoples.
> You with your arm redeemed your people,
>> the children of Jacob and Joseph....
>
> Your way was through the sea,
>> your path through the great waters;
>> yet your footprints were unseen.
> You led your people like a flock
>> by the hand of Moses and Aaron.

—Psalm 77:13-15, 19-20

The psalm ends without resolution, but it does show resolve. In much the same way as Job, Asaph determines to approach his difficulties from a new perspective. Instead of asking the subjective question, "Why does God refuse to show himself to me?" he changes the subject to an objective one. "Who is God?"

From there the answer becomes apparent. The God of the narrative is the God who works wonders, who demonstrates his might among his people, who redeems the children of Jacob and Joseph,[46] and who leads his people like a flock across the Red Sea under Moses and Aaron. Asaph must praise, and the last three sections fulfill his unstated vow of praise.

Conclusion

By and large, modern Western culture, including Christian culture, has lost the ability to understand suffering as anything but a problem to be eliminated. From this perspective, life becomes a formula wrapped with a bow. We spend our lives looking for our personal *happily ever after*. When Asaph tried, he came up empty. In the end, he had to reach back to his faith foundations.

Centuries later, when Jesus prayed in the Garden of Gethsemane just before he went to trial and crucifixion, he begged God to let the cup of suffering he was about to endure to pass from him. In the end, God called him to carry on, and Jesus took his mission willingly.

Believers throughout history have had to deal with severe difficulties. Psalm 77 shows how hollow pat answers can be. Asaph teaches profoundly important lessons with this psalm.

- Sometimes easy solutions will elude us.
- Sometimes talking about the joy of the Lord will seem like sawdust in our mouths.
- Sometimes our only viable course of action lacks a positive resolution.
- Sometimes, instead of seeking resolution, we must determine to build resolve.

If easy answers eluded Asaph and Jesus, perhaps the average Christian's expectations for such things are shortsighted. Asaph shows us that we are allowed to struggle in our faith. We are not "unspiritual" if we find ourselves unable to come up with an immediate solution.

Remember that in the Psalms, praise lives side by side with grief, loss, and anger. The journey back to praise becomes meaningful because it involves deliverance from these things. In 1 Chronicles 16:41, Asaph, Heman, and Jeduthun were to give thanks to the LORD, for his steadfast love endures forever. Praise was never so one-dimensional as to forget their sorrow. God never meant for us to use praise as the replacement drug of choice for our anxiety. He demonstrates his steadfast love by going through the anxiety with us.

Journal Entry

What do you lament? How do you feel about it? What are your feelings toward God? _____

_____

_____

_____

Douglas Knox

Where can you go to place a personal anchor hold for your faith? What can you affirm about God to be objectively true? _____

_____

_____

_____

CHAPTER 8

Psalm 88
It's Me, Lord. Remember?

The people on the coast
are beginning to drink sea water.
We here in the mountains
don't even have sea water to drink.
Dear Lord send the rain.
—Haitian Peasant Prayer[47]

During the months after my first wife Marie died, I found solace on the water. Throughout the summer and fall, from two to four times a week, I would take my canoe to a boat launch near my home and paddle up the Black Fork River. Marie's death was still fresh, and paddling allowed me to satisfy my need for solitude, meditation, and exercise.

One of my most memorable trips took place that November. The weather had been unusually rainy for the late fall, and the river was high. I enjoyed the challenge of canoeing in high water. I would paddle until the current matched my paddling speed. Then I would turn around and coast back. The physical exertion took my mind away from the grief for a few minutes.

This day the river was the highest it had been in my canoeing experience, and the lure was irresistible. The paddle up the Black Fork was challenging, and the effort felt gratifying. About a mile and a half from my launching point, I came to one of the bends in the river, where a runnel cut through the woods. During normal river levels, the channel was too shallow to paddle, but it became passable in higher water. On this day, the current made the channel the only safe choice. I took it without thinking about the consequences of hitting the even heavier water above.

When I steered back into the main part of the river, the current was already near my paddling speed, but I felt good. I had to see how much farther I could go. That distance turned out to be only a few dozen yards. I managed to paddle about twenty feet past a tree that had fallen a few days before, but that was all. Try as I might, I could not make any more progress upstream.

Satisfied, I started to turn around for the return trip. By the time I made a quarter turn, however, I realized I was going to collide with the downed tree broadside. I expected to experience a few moments' inconvenience while I pushed myself away from the foliage.

The river had a different idea. The moment my canoe touched the tree, it flipped. I panicked and threw my legs out, and my foot lodged between the gun whale and the cross bar. The canoe now was upside down, and I was in the water, with my foot caught. I fought to keep my head above the surface. To free my leg I would have to go under the water, but I was hyperventilating. Until I could control my panic, I was helpless.

Then a thought shot into my consciousness like an arrow. The days had been so dark. Grief bore down daily, without letup. My church was unable to minister to me. Even my daughters had lashed out at me in anger. I felt alienated from everyone. Suddenly the anticipated violent end transformed into an opportunity. How easy it would be to let myself go, to allow my head to slip under the surface. The few moments of terror would fade into unconsciousness and then to nothing. My pain would be gone, and no one would be the wiser. My death would look like an accidental drowning.

Yes, even Christians fall into despair. And sometimes they contemplate suicide.

Psalm 88 and the Descent into Despair

In the Chronicles, Asaph, Heman, and Jeduthun are "chosen and expressly named to give thanks to the LORD, for his steadfast love endures forever" (1 Chronicles 16:41). These men understood that giving thanks to the LORD was a much broader experience than closing their repertoire to anything but praise songs. Giving thanks in the biblical sense involves our whole range of emotional experience. Our dark periods matter, because they make the need to return to praise all the more urgent.

Psalm 88 proves that even our depression matters to God. The sons of

Korah are responsible for the text, while Heman sets the musical notation. It neither gives thanks nor celebrates the LORD's steadfast love. The psalm struggles with emptiness. As the musician for the psalm, Heman was called to write the music of despair. I believe the sons of Korah sought his musical interpretation for much the same reason that Asaph asked Jeduthun to put Psalm 77 to music.

Since we lack outside background for Psalm 88, we must derive what we know from the text. This psalm moves through many themes, all dark. We will examine it thematically.

The Deathlike Grip of Despair

Despair is a view from the bottom of a hole. Even the word *up* may resist description. Only the hole exists, and life passes without visible bearings. Because of the emotional confusion involved with despair, ordinary tasks involving the will become impossible. Therefore, when well-meaning friends tell the person in despair, "Just trust God," the words come off with all the comfort of an acid bath.

For a person who has exhausted all the standard formulas, God has gone off the grid. He is nowhere *to* trust. Without this lifeline, believing God is the same as trusting nothing at all.

Psalm 88 is a psalm written during a time of despair. God has become a tormentor rather than a comforter. The psalm begins with a cry.

> O LORD, God of my salvation;
> I cry out day and night before you.
> Let my prayer come before you;
> incline your ear to my cry.

—Psalm 88:1-2

The picture is one of endless moral darkness—days and nights spent in crying out to God while he remains silent. Images of death dominate the psalmist's landscape:

> For my soul is full of troubles,
> my life draws near to Sheol.

I am counted among those who go down to the pit;
    I am a man who has no strength,
like one set loose among the dead,
    like the slain that lie in the grave,
like those whom you remember no more,
    for they are cut off from your hand.

—Psalm 88:3-5

These words constitute the language of abandonment. They lack either hope or option. The three similes in verse 5 show the psalmist's state of mind. Despair feels like death and abandonment.

- "Like one set loose among the dead" attests to Heman's emotional state. He is alive but helpless, doomed to live among those who know nothing.
- "Like the slain that lie in the grave," develops the picture further. This simile brings the psalmist even nearer to the dead, as though he shares the mass grave with them. He is both physically and morally abandoned.
- "Like those whom you remember no more," takes the picture to the edge and shows the end that the psalmist sees for himself. These words do not mean that God has momentarily forgotten him or pushed him into the background. The word *remember* is an important one in the Bible, far more significant than a calendar reminder like, "Cub Scouts Tuesday, 7:00 p.m." The term signifies God's particular care and intervention for someone. Its meaning is closer to, "Mark me for your special favor." When someone utters the words, "Remember me," that person's situation is dire.

For one who has experienced this kind of emptiness, failure to remember is worse than forgetting. If a husband should miss his anniversary, he can make up for it. He may have to up the ante to include dinner, a spa visit, and roses delivered to a hotel room, but his wife knows his breach was unintentional.

But what if the day comes and goes, and even after he has opened the card from his wife, he does nothing? Neglect in this degree signifies the failure to consider his wife to be significant enough to notice or care. Apathy like this cripples a marriage.

For the psalmist, God is on the verge of this kind of apathy. God's abandonment has left him indistinguishable from the dead. He finds himself removed from God's covenantal care. He is outside of God's *hesed*, God's steadfast, enduring love. God remains apathetic. The words "remember no more" signify absolute and final abandonment.

The section concludes with three complaints directed at the LORD:

> You have put me in the depths of the pit,
>   in the regions dark and deep.
> Your wrath lies heavy upon me,
>   and you overwhelm me with all your waves.
>
> —Psalm 88:6-7

The Loss of Friends

Close friends are essential during a crisis. When all else fails, the comfort from a steady friend can be priceless. Here, however, the writer's friends and close companions have abandoned him, making him an outcast. He writes,

> You have caused my companions to shun me;
>   you have made me a horror to them.
>
> —Psalm 88:8

> You have caused my beloved and my friend to shun me;
>   my companions have become darkness.
>
> —Psalm 88:18

Both verses begin, "You have caused...." This language is directed *at* God rather than *to* him. Such language is typical in psalms written on behalf of the people (for example, Psalms 44:9-16; 80:4-6; 89:38-45), but is rare in the laments of the individual, such as this psalm. The reason involves the writers' sense of reverence toward God. Ancient cultures did not share our modern obsession with the individual. While the writers did not hesitate to heap blame on God when the issue involved their people as a whole, the individual was another matter entirely.

The difference in the way the people appealed to God individually as opposed to their pleas for their people as a whole was subtle but important. Challenging God to act was permissible for an individual, but blaming him crossed a moral line. According to Westermann, *"The complaint against God* is dominant in the lament of the people....Its most frequent form is the question directed at God, usually introduced with "Why?"[48] By contrast, in the laments of the individual, "The accusatory question directed at God recedes into the background. It is a risk no longer taken."[49]

The psalmist's loss of friends appears to be a result of his difficulty rather than a cause for it. In other psalms, for example, David speaks about betrayal (see Psalms 41:9 and 55:12-14). The author of Psalm 88 is silent. His friends have abandoned him *after* his abandonment by God.

The stress becomes almost unbearable. In the book of Job, for example, Job shifts the focal point for justice from God's throne to himself. The psalmists are careful to respect the boundary between God-centered truth and human-centered desire. But when the writer of Psalm 88 twice declares, *"You have caused* my companions to shun me," and, *"You have caused* my beloved and my friend to shun me," he approaches that line.

Endlessness in Suffering

We find one other factor from the context.—duration. Rightly or wrongly, the psalmist remembers far more suffering than joy. He writes,

> Afflicted and close to death from my youth up,
> I suffer your terrors; I am helpless.

> —Psalm 88:15

His relationship with his God has been a difficult one throughout his life. We have to wonder what difficulties he has had to endure.

Death

The author says a great deal about death.

> Do you work wonders for the dead?
>   Do the departed rise up to praise you? *Selah*
> Is your steadfast love declared in the grave,
>   or your faithfulness in Abaddon [Destruction]?
> Are your wonders known in the darkness,
>   or your righteousness in the land of forgetfulness?

—Psalm 88:10-12

The Psalms speak little about eternal life, which leads some modern scholars to believe that the idea entered into the biblical writers' thinking later in history. The issue here is not *whether* the psalmists believed in an afterlife. That idea had been embedded in Egyptian theology for centuries and doubtless was known to the Hebrews. The issue for the Hebrews is the LORD's *hesed*, his ever-present covenant kindness. Without hope for the LORD's *hesed,* life was hopeless. Westermann explains,

> [T]he praise of God in Israel never became...separated from the rest of existence, in a separate realm, that had become independent of the history of the people and of the individual. Rather it occupied a central place in the total life of the individual and the people before God, as for instance the concept of faith does for us.[50]

Westermann goes on to say, "The possibility that there could also be life in which there was no praise, life that did *not* praise God, does not enter into the picture here."[51] In other words, for the ancient Hebrew, to be alive was to be involved in a daily relationship with the LORD in which the person was able to offer up public praise to his creator and redeemer for his *hesed.* To die meant to be separated from this most basic element of life. Quoting Westermann again, "The conclusion is not expressed in the O.T. but it must be drawn. There cannot be such a thing as a true life without praise. Praising and no longer praising are related to each other as are living and no longer living."[52]

King Hezekiah, the eighth-century-BC king of Judah, bears this out.

When he became seriously ill, the prophet Isaiah told him to set his house in order because he about to die (Isaiah 38:1). Hezekiah begged the LORD to heal him, and the LORD sent Isaiah back to him with his answer. God had granted the king fifteen more years. Upon hearing this, Hezekiah offered a prayer of praise to the LORD. Thematically, it bears a strong resemblance to the plea in Psalm 88.

> I said, I shall not see the LORD,
>> the LORD in the land of the living;
> I shall look on man no more
>> among the inhabitants of the world....
>
> For sheol does not thank you;
>> death does not praise you;
> those who go down to the pit do not hope
>> for your faithfulness.
> *The living, the living, he thanks you,*
>> *as I do this day:*
> *the father makes known to the children*
>> *your faithfulness.*

—Isaiah 38:11, 18-19, emphasis added

The opening line of Isaiah 38:19, "The living, the living, he thanks you," marks this point in the Hebrew mind. The dead are unable to fulfill their fundamental reason for living, to give praise to God for his works. Similarly, the purpose of the father is to declare God's faithfulness to his children. Psalm 118 also expresses this thought.

> I shall not die, but I shall live,
>> *and recount the deeds of the LORD.*

—Psalm 118:17

That hope is absent in Psalm 88, and the writer cannot bear to face life without it.

The Finger Hold in the Cliff: Positive
Faith Indicators in the Psalm

In the classic lament form, this psalm contains a *vav*-adversative, the marker by which the psalmists illustrate their change in thematic direction. Here, however, the *vav*-adversative does not signal a sudden sense of assurance. It builds the psalmist's complaint by marking the contrast between the dead, who offer neither praise nor prayer, and the writer's unceasing plea to the LORD. In other words, he refuses to give up. The literal translation of the first line in verse 13 is, "But I—to you, O LORD, I cry..."

In spite of his unceasing cry, the author remains in darkness. In the last verse, quoted above, the author finds himself consigned to darkness. One way of translating the last line bears a strong similarity to a line from the 1964 Simon and Garfunkel song, "The Sound of Silence." The closing of the psalm can read, "Darkness is my only friend." The psalm leaves the writer in his pain.

Conclusion

As dark as this psalm is, we can conclude with positive applications. The first has to do with depression itself. Contrary to popular thinking, depression by itself is not an automatic pointer to some hidden flaw in our spiritual life. Even righteous people can feel abandoned. We do not have to feel guilty when we are unable to think happy thoughts. To state the truth another way, the Bible does not contain a sliding scale that reads "Happy/Spiritual" on one end and "Depressed/Unspiritual" on the other. Some difficulties are just too deep to fix with a simple word.

In some cases, depression is physiological. Our bodies are intricate. They are God's creation, "fearfully and wonderfully made" (Psalm 139:14). But we live in a fallen universe, and biological systems can fall into disarray. I suffer from mild depression and know many who suffer far more intensely. In cases like these, we should realize that "mental" illness implies no more sense of failure than physical illness.

Sometimes, however, sin turns out to be its cause. Probably the most well-known biblical example is King David's abuse of power with Bathsheba. The account of the incident, along with Nathan the prophet's confrontation over the incident, can be found in 2 Samuel chapters 11-12. David's song of confession after Nathan's speech occurs in Psalm 51.[53]

If sin is the cause for depression, we need to deal with the issue appropriately. And that means gently if at all possible, without giving in to the temptation to create class distinctions between "righteous" people versus "sinful" people. The Apostle Paul writes, "Brothers, if anyone is caught in any transgression, you who are spiritual should restore him in a spirit of gentleness. Keep watch on yourself, lest you too be tempted" (Galatians 6:1-2).

If someone mourns, the Bible calls us to cry with that person. The Apostle Paul writes, "Rejoice with those who rejoice, weep with those who weep" (Romans 12:15). Grief after a loss is normal.

Finally, we must say a word about the question of suicide. Despair at this level is a serious matter. In some cases, even faithful people resort to suicide. During the weeks following the 9/11 attacks, Attorney General John Ashcroft appointed Kenneth Feinberg to administer a newly created September 11th Victim Compensation Fund. Feinberg assumed sole responsibility and discretion in determining the amount of compensation that would go to each of the victims or their families. He administered each of the more than five thousand claims and made every attempt to handle them with the delicacy they deserved.

One case involved a widow whose husband died in the World Trade Center. To make matters worse, the widow's son had committed suicide. This was a religious family. The woman's attorney expressed the pathos of her case during her hearing.

> [This spouse and mother] is a steady church attender and has, I hope, an unshakable faith in God. But she called me after the death of her son and she said, "How am I supposed to be able to accept?" She alluded to the biblical Job, God testing one with one onslaught after another. I think she has been tested almost beyond endurance.[54]

We are safe to assume the son's suicide came about as a result of his faith crisis. No drugs or wrongdoing were involved. This crisis occurred after one of the most violent acts imaginable, and the son chose the inescapable escape from his despair.

I lack the background to comment on the psychological aspects of suicide, and I will not make that attempt. I cannot condemn the young man. As I wrote at the beginning of this chapter, after I lost Marie, I came within seconds of making the same decision.

Psalm 88 ultimately can give us hope in the face of suicide because it shows that we are neither alone in our situation, nor are we necessarily the cause of the situation. In some cases, circumstances prove to be hopeless. In cases like those, we need to offer sympathy, prayer, and assistance, rather than platitudes or too-easy solutions. As the book of Job showed, depression does not automatically lead to sin as a cause. Author Philip Yancey draws this observation on Psalm 88 in his book, *The Bible Jesus Read*.

> Kathleen Norris writes of a Catholic sister who counsels troubled women—displaced homemakers, abused wives, women returning to college after years away—and finds that Psalms offers a helpful pattern of expressing rage that the church often tries to repress. "Bear it up; keep smiling; suffering makes you strong," say some spiritual advisors—but not the psalmists. They do not rationalize anger away or give general advice about pain; rather, they express emotion vividly and loudly, directing their feelings primarily at God.[55]

Individually, the psalms stand as testimonies to the writers' faith. Whether they offer praise or complaint, they never abandon their trust in God. In this psalm, the writer's opening words are, "O LORD, God of my salvation" (Psalm 88:1). The mere fact that he calls out to the God who has saved him is a testimony to the psalmist's trust in his God. The writer understands God's faithfulness. To use Yancey's term, the psalmist rages against the God of his salvation because he knows his God will hear him.

Ultimately his complaint in the last verse, "You have caused my beloved and my friend to shun me; / my companions have become darkness," points to his faith. His complaint rises out of his unstated confession of trust. God has entered into an unbreakable covenant with his people. No matter how difficult the situation is, he continues to appeal to the God of the covenant.

Even in the darkest times, the book of Psalms maintains the connection between praise and lament. It understands the two to be interrelated. Because of that, the Psalms recognize that deliverance is not always just a prayer—or praise—away. The faith depicted here is deeper than spiritual button pushing. Each psalm is part of the spectrum of emotion between prayer and praise, and they all seek to be able to praise God for deliverance.

Journal Entry

In the quote above, Yancey mentions "rage that the church often tries to repress."[56] This exercise will call you to express your rage rather than suppress it. In the spirit of Psalm 88, how would you describe your experience in the following areas—including rage?

Your descent into despair: _____

_____

_____

_____

The deathlike experience of despair: _____

_____

_____

_____

Endlessness in suffering: _____

_____

_____

_____

Death itself: _____

_____

_____

_____

Your finger hold on the cliff while you wait for God to do something:

_____

_____

_____

CHAPTER 9

Psalm 73
The Shape of Grief

In this world, the bad guys can win.[57]

When our three daughters were in grade school, Marie and I found a Bible-based character-building audio series. The series included both dramatized biblical narratives and modern stories that taught moral lessons to children. The stories featured children and teenagers who faced various ethical dilemmas. They placed the characters in any number of challenging difficulties, such as greed, pride, anger, laziness, embarrassment, or a dozen others. Nor were the lead characters squeaky clean. Often they would make a wrong choice, only to find themselves backtracking to correct their errors later. Even though our girls listened to them repeatedly, neither Marie nor I ever grew tired of hearing the lessons.

After a while, however, I began to notice a pattern in the moral lessons. They all contained one or more unstated but definite assumptions.

- Right moral choices were difficult.
- Wrong moral choices were far easier to make.
- In some cases, bad moral choices erred more on the side of convenience than actual evil. Without exception, they offered an immediate but ultimately less satisfying solution to a genuine need.
- If a person did make a wrong moral choice, he or she would have a chance to rectify the matter, but the task would be made more difficult than it would have been otherwise.

The characters that made wise moral decisions often suffered, but their inconvenience was temporary. The stories always ended happily. In other words, the story series presented a universe just like the one that governed Job's three friends. The ultimate message was one that faithful people have believed from the beginning of time:

- Wrong choices always end in adverse consequences.
- God always rewards right moral choices in a way that proves the superiority of the more difficult option.
- The good guys always win.

Psalm 73 and the Myth of the Blessed "Righteous Life"

The moral assumptions in the children's stories range far beyond children's imaginations. Adults hold these expectations as well. At some time or another, each one of us dons our spiritual invincibility cape, stands on the train tracks, and braces ourselves to stop the rolling train. Of course, the train rolls on without as much as a shudder, while we find ourselves sprawled and broken at the side of the tracks, wondering what happened.

In the real world, good morals sometimes result in adverse consequences.

The situation often comes to a head when children enter into young adulthood. High school and college challenge students' tidy moral lessons about life. Often, the crisis becomes too difficult to reconcile, and once-faithful young people abandon their beliefs altogether. The same end almost occurred with Asaph. Psalm 73 marks his autobiographical odyssey. The psalm describes his personal crisis, his readiness to walk out on everything he had believed, and his final fight to reestablish his faith.

Asaph's journey looks like a giant letter U. He begins in moral free fall, but in the middle of the psalm calls himself to think with discipline once again. The second half of the psalm describes his journey back to reason.

The Two Themes in the Psalm, (verses 1-3)

Asaph begins with the two themes that summarize the psalm. The first occurs in the opening verse.

> Surely God is good to those in Israel,
> to those who are pure in heart.

> —Psalm 73:1

Asaph's definition of the word "good" in this statement is absolute. God is good to his people at all times and in all circumstances. Even when the bad guys win, God remains good to his people. God's indestructible goodness becomes the framework that guides Asaph's emotions in the second half of the psalm and the one that ultimately lifts him out of his despair.

A conflicting theme occurs in verses 2-3. This theme is the darker of the two, and the one that will dominate the first half of the psalm.

> But as for me, my feet had almost slipped;
> I had nearly lost my foothold.
> For I envied the arrogant
> when I saw the prosperity of the wicked.

> —Psalm 73:2-3

Asaph's Descent into Envy, (verses 4-12)

Asaph's confession is remarkable in its honesty. In effect he says, "I envied the rich. Not just the wealthy, but the arrogant wealthy who had made their gains by exploitation." These are the people who have it all at any expense. In their minds, they are the world. Those beneath them lack the merit to count.

Asaph's moral crisis grows even deeper when he examines the manner of thinking in the unrighteous rich. As he peels back the layers in the exploiters' reasoning, new revelations send ever deeper shock waves through his brain.

The outer layers are unsurprising. First, wealth drives the wicked rich to pride. Then pride takes a darker turn.

> Therefore pride is their necklace:
> violence covers them as a garment.

> —Psalm 73:6

Asaph's description features metaphors that use clothing. A necklace is an accessory, something that one shows off. The boastful rich sport their pride this way. A garment, on the other hand, does far more to define the person. For example, if we see a man walking down Main Street with an overcoat and a tie, we draw a precise mental picture of him. He might be an attorney or a businessman, but whatever his particular career is, we picture him as a professional.

Another man wearing a camouflage coat and a stocking cap conjures up another picture, while a man in a biker vest and a steel helmet gives us a different picture entirely. Among the unjust rich, Asaph observes, the universal defining garment is violence. They have become rich by exploitation.

Asaph's second observation looks deeper into their mindsets, and the picture is ugly.

> Their eyes swell out through fatness;
> their hearts overflow with follies.
> They scoff and speak with malice;
> loftily they threaten opposition.

> —Psalm 73:7-8

While wealth itself is neither good nor bad, excessive wealth taken for granted can lead to complacency regarding its blindness toward others' needs.

Third and last, the pride of the arrogant wealthy begins to drive them toward an amoral path in their thinking. They assume God is either unconcerned about them or unaware of their deeds. Given Asaph's description, this is the most shocking development of all.

> They set their mouths against the heavens,
> and their tongue struts through the earth....

> And they say, "How can God know?
> Is there knowledge in the Most High?"
> These are the wicked;
> always at ease, they increase in riches.

> —Psalm 73:9, 11

Envy is never just a single shade of green. It is multi-hued. We turn it one way, and it seems loathsome. When we turn it another, it beckons us to do whatever we must to join the privileged few. Asaph is honest enough to show us his multi-hued envy that, at this moment, is driving him to madness. His situation, compelled by reason and feeling at the same time, is a universal gut reaction. Each of us has felt this way at one time or another.

The Bottom of a Dry Well, (verse 13)

The question, "How can God know?" stretches Asaph's belief system beyond its limits. His personal theology has proven inadequate to address this issue. Without a solution, he comes near to abandoning his faith. He describes his conclusion regarding his faith this way:

> All in vain have I kept my heart clean
> and washed my hands in innocence.
> For all the day long I have been stricken
> and rebuked every morning.

> —Psalm 73:13-14

Our sense of morality forms our behavioral boundary. For Asaph, who holds firm moral boundaries, bad-mouthing God is unthinkable. The Third Commandment says, "You shall not take the name of the LORD your God in vain, for the LORD will not hold him guiltless who takes his name in vain" (Exodus 20:7). Asaph has honored the Law of God, and he expects God to honor him.

Then he sees the wicked blaspheme with impunity. No excess is too high. No exploitation is too severe. The realization pulls Asaph in opposite directions simultaneously. From his moral perspective, the arrogant are repugnant to him. At the same time, while he stands to the side with empty-handed moral superiority, the amoral wealthy bulge with riches. Their wealth begins to batter his moral boundary. Therefore, when we read the line, "All in vain have I kept my heart clean, / and washed my hands in innocence," we need to read it at face value. In flat terms, it says, "The faith formula has failed, so I am ready to abandon my moral and behavioral boundaries."

Here is a man who has served as worship leader for united Israel under David and Solomon. Twelve Psalms bear his name. He is one of the most spiritually upright people in the land, and yet he is ready to walk out on his faith. We find ourselves asking how such an established leader in his faith could contemplate this kind of abandonment.

The remarkable truth about this psalm is less about Asaph in his fall than it is about Asaph in his honesty. Anyone who has thought seriously about issues that conflict with the faith faces dilemmas like this. The remarkable thing about this psalm is that Asaph is willing to confess his confusion out loud. He is angry. His entire concept of right and wrong has collapsed.

Asaph's Logical Choices

At this point, Asaph has reached the bottom of his descent. His theology has crashed head-on with reality, leaving him with only two logical choices. Either he can take the easy way out of the dilemma, or he can take the difficult way through it. Each carries consequences.

Suppose Asaph decides to abandon his faith. This decision is far bigger than a two-week resignation notice from his choirmaster position. First, since he had decided that his faith has failed to work, he has to make a clean break from it. He cannot hold it at arm's length until he decides what his final decision will be. He will have to walk away from the worship he has embraced all his life.

The second consequence follows directly from the first. If Asaph is to be consistent in his new affirmation of the lifestyle he loathes, he will have to deny the moral framework on which he has built his faith.

This issue strikes at the essence of the questions posed by the amoral rich. "How can God know? / Is there knowledge in the Most High?" (verse 11). The people whose pride is their necklace, whose eyes swell out through their fatness, consider themselves to be their internal standard. No one else matters.

To join them, Asaph would have to set his speech against heavenly principles, strut through the earth in his pride, and shake his fist at God's apparent ignorance of the situation on the earth (verses 9, 11). He would have to contradict everything he has stood for in his life. The easy way out takes him to betrayal.

Asaph's other logical choice is to wrestle with the difficulties in the problem as one who has embraced a belief in God and his goodness. This choice has consequences as well, because it drives him straight into the theodicy issue, the quest to explain the evil in the world against the backdrop of God's essential goodness. Asaph must build a convincing defense for his choice to stay with his faith if he is to be able to defend his choice before the world. Ultimately the reward is worth the work.

Faith in Dialogue with Itself, (verse 15)

Interestingly, Asaph's course of action chooses him rather than the reverse. Immediately after his cynical conclusion, "For all the day long I have been stricken / and rebuked every morning" (verse 14), he comes to this realization:

> If I had said, "I will speak thus,"
> I would have betrayed the generation of your children.
>
> —Psalm 73:15

This statement shows faith in dialogue with itself. The very belief system Asaph wants to reject stands up against him and says, "You cannot do that."

Why?

Because he would be required to deny his faith system.

His reasoning is circular in the strongest sense of the word. At the same time, it is the most powerful argument imaginable to protect his faith. The reason goes back to the nature of what is most abhorrent to Asaph regarding the exploitative rich. The arrogant rich cannot feel compassion because their wealth requires them to exploit the poor. If Asaph had carried out his threat to join them, his act would have constituted a betrayal of those who looked to him for a vindication of their belief.

The realization becomes a personal crisis for Asaph, and it stops him in his tracks. While he may have been willing to betray his own beliefs, he cannot allow his personal crisis to demolish the faith of those who watch him.

This decision ultimately brings Asaph back to terms with his faith. When he faces the bare-bones choice between faith that defies explanation and cynicism that destroys compassion, the needs of the faithful speak to him. Asaph does not make his decision because he has come to a new sense of understanding. He chooses his course of action based on purpose. This verse becomes the driving impulse for his determination to side with those who walk in faith.

A Dilemma Too Difficult to Ponder, (verses 16-17)

Once he comes to his realization in verse 15, Asaph proves his character. He demonstrates his identity by choosing principle over expedience. At the same time, however, his choice requires him to commit to a line of thinking for which he has yet to find an adequate defense. The next two verses, though, chart the turning point of the psalm. They begin in despair and end with a glimmer of hope.

> But when I thought how to understand this,
>> it seemed to me a wearisome task,
> until I went into the sanctuary of God;
>> then I discerned their end.

—Psalm 73:16-17

In the first two lines, his gaze remains downward. No matter how deeply he digs, he will not find the answer in himself alone. He becomes lost in himself. Verse 17 marks the change of direction: "...*until* I went into the sanctuary of God; / *then* I discerned their end." From this point, he looks to God for moral guidance.

The sheer power of turning our gaze to the God who has the answers rather than groping in the dark to find the answers on our own is remarkable. When my oldest daughter graduated from high school, she received an invitation to work for a summer camp at a state park for six weeks. Because she and the other counselors would be working with kids from juvenile detention, their names had to remain anonymous, even from each other. My daughter was assigned the nickname, Bean.

The atmosphere turned out to be very political, but she was locked in a contract. Because of the criminal records among the teenagers, the counselors were disallowed to use cell phones or any media. They could send and receive postal mail, however, and my daughter and I wrote back and forth almost daily. To encourage her, I made up a cartoon character named Beanie—a kidney bean with Mickey Mouse arms and legs, sunglasses, a cowboy hat, and an attitude. Whenever my daughter sent news back, I would draw a Beanie cartoon to illustrate it.

By the fourth week, my daughter knew that her efforts to release herself from the contract had failed. The realization that she had to remain at the camp for the last two weeks of her contract drove her to the darkest despair I had seen. I drew a cartoon with Beanie shackled to the camp sign. Darkness dominates the right side of the scene, but on the left, a cross breaks through the clouds in the sky. Light pours from the cross. Beanie, sitting on the ground weeping, looks up. The cross lights her face, and as she looks at it, she sees her source of hope.

My point was simple. You may lack an answer now, but God knows your grief. Set your eyes on the hope before you, because hope is our legitimate source of joy. It becomes the basis for praise when other sources remain invisible. When Asaph enters the sanctuary, he experiences a similar revelation.

Up from Ground Zero

The temple lacks any magical powers. Asaph's moment of resolution occurs when he realizes *what* God owns and what he plans to do with it. God's purpose sees beyond the immediate to a more distant goal that involves the ultimate reestablishment of justice.

In Asaph's words, "...then I discerned their end" (verse 17). The unrighteous rich may go to their graves in comfort, but their demise marks the close of their lifestyles. Their fates are in God's hands. Though they are ignorant of the fact, they tumble out of control toward their end. Asaph writes,

> Truly you set them in slippery places;
>   you make them fall into ruin.
> How they are destroyed in a moment,
>   swept away utterly by terrors!
> Like a dream when one awakes,

O Lord, when you rouse yourself, you despise them as
phantoms.

—Psalm 73:18-20

Asaph's resolution does not stop with his insight about the wicked
man's ultimate fate. His confession about his thinking is far more personal.

When my soul was embittered,
    when I was pricked in heart,
I was brutish and ignorant,
    I was like a beast toward you.

—Psalm 73:21-22

His depiction of his beast-like behavior is a vivid one. We can imagine
an untamed animal in a cage. It thrashes about in a rage, always bent on
escape and never caring whether it injures itself in its futile attempts.

Asaph's Commitment to Praise, (verses 23-28)

The turning point for the psalm occurs in verse 23, with the *vav*-adversative
pointing to the writer. The verse reads literally,

But I—I am ever with you;
    you grasp [the] hand—my right hand.

—Psalm 73:23, author's translation

In the ancient world, the right hand signified the privileged position.
Asaph's point of praise, then, comes from the realization that, unlike the
wicked rich, he occupies a place of honor at his God's side. Once he
understands this truth, three corollaries fall into place:

- First, he realizes the truth about the wicked and their inevitable destruction (verses 18-20).
- Second, he sees the truth about his heart, (verses 21-22). His ranting has made him resemble a wild, senseless animal.
- Finally, he is able to grasp he truth concerning God's faithfulness toward his covenant people (verses 23-26). Now he sees clearly enough to engage in praise.

The psalm closes in praise and also in pain. The wicked still prosper, and Asaph still suffers. Yet he can praise God in the midst of pain. The following bullet points quote the closing verses and comment on them.

- Verse 23: "Nevertheless, I am continually with you; / you hold my right hand." Even when he was in grief and thrashing about like an untamed animal, he remained in God's right hand. We who belong to God are as unable to escape his care for us as the wicked are to escape their slide toward judgment.
- Verse 24: "You guide me with your counsel, / and afterward you will receive me to glory." Two characteristics separate Asaph from the amoral rich. One, he experiences God's guiding counsel. Of course the amoral gladly live without counsel, so this hardly seems like an advantage. But when the rich become jealous because someone else is richer, they have nowhere to turn in their jealousy. Two, beyond the immediate lifetime benefits, Asaph knows God will receive him to glory. Earlier, when he complained that the amoral rich experience "no pangs in their death" (verse 4), he neglected to look beyond death. Death is the great equalizer. Regardless of our wealth, we all will leave the world naked. Those who die with a secure knowledge of the Lord have an advocate when they face the final terrors.
- Verse 25: "Whom have I in heaven but you? / And there is nothing on earth that I desire besides you." Now, Asaph can put his priorities in order. Our knowledge of God is more than a crutch. It balances us when we run into crisis.
- Verse 26: "My flesh and my heart may fail, but God is the strength of my heart and my portion forever." The rich remain rich, and they still strut in front of the world. Sometimes that fact is too painful to

bear. But when we revere God as our chief possession, everything else ultimately falls back into focus.

Conclusion: Lesson Learned

The psalm ends with these words:

> For behold, those who are far from you shall perish;
>   you put an end to everyone who is unfaithful to you.
> But for me it is good to be near God;
>   I have made the Lord God my refuge,
>   that I may tell of all your works.

—Psalm 73:27-28

Asaph completes his journey with two conclusions. From a factual standpoint, those who are far from God gain nothing when they reach their end. They perish like everyone else. Unlike the righteous, however, their demise will mean their destruction.

From a moral perspective, Asaph reaches a new sense of commitment. He has made the sovereign God his refuge so that he can testify to his deeds. Such praise is the chief joy for the ancient Hebrews. For Asaph, it includes telling the moral tale of his own fall and rising again.

Journal Entry

Comparative thinking is virtually impossible to avoid. In what areas have I shifted my focus to the way my living compares with others? _____

_____

_____

_____

How can I place definite value on making "the LORD God my refuge, / that I may tell of all your works"? _____

_____

_____

_____

CHAPTER 10

Psalm 109
The Surprising Path to Forgiveness

Thought is never static; pain often is.[58]

Introduction

Forgiveness is a crucially important issue for all Christians. The clause in Jesus' model prayer for his disciples, "Forgive us our debts, as we also have forgiven our debtors" (Matthew 6:12), calls us to practice the same generosity that we expect from God. This is a difficult task. All of us will struggle with forgiveness at some point in our lives.

The problem becomes even more difficult when we consider the cursing psalms, known by their more technical name, imprecatory psalms. The moment we encounter a psalm that calls for God to strike down the writer's enemy, its world crashes into Jesus' world of forgiveness. The questions are immediate, and they are urgent.

- Why does the Bible include such radically different responses to personal evil?
- Does Jesus' doctrine of forgiveness allow such speech, or should we exclude psalms like this from our consideration?
- If we do decide to exclude the cursing psalms, on what basis do we do so?

Many have argued that the cursing psalms are Old Testament, a now obsolete and abandoned part of the Bible, but this ignores the high regard with which the New Testament views the Hebrew Scriptures. This chapter will defend the position that genuine forgiveness is more than a mere dismissal of a wrong. For forgiveness to be complete, it must involve an honest assessment of the evil followed by the act of giving the matter to God. A proper understanding of the cursing psalms ultimately harmonizes them with what Jesus says about forgiveness.

The Myth of "Forgive and Forget"

The almost universal contemporary understanding of forgiveness, at least among the religious, is summarized by the three words, "Forgive and forget." The statement implies graciousness, finality, and obedience to Jesus' call to "forgive our debtors." It also raises questions about justice and satisfaction, especially if the offense is a serious one.

1. Is "Forgive and forget" just a one-sided demand that ignores the need for personal closure?
2. Does the requirement invalidate any wish we might have for justice?
3. When the first and only response we are allowed to voice is forgiveness, is that the same as saying the offense is inconsequential?
4. Can forgiveness be genuine if we are disallowed to process the wrong that has damaged us?
5. What do we do when the effective forgive-and-forget counsel looks less like comfort and more like somebody's idea of a Monopoly game caricature? "Go directly to forgiveness. Do not pass *Go*. Do not collect $200."

These questions are genuine. Anyone who has been wounded by someone's wrong act, only to have to deal with the pain on his own, knows that the presumed "spiritual" response leaves a lot more emotional debris than spiritual fruit in its wake. I know of a case where a pastoral counselor tried to convince a sexual molestation victim that her first and only duty was to forgive the person who had violated her, without giving her the chance to process the issues herself. He used the book of Hosea the prophet to leverage the woman he counseled. His misuse of the book as a proof text requires us to examine his assumptions. The book begins with these words:

> When the LORD first spoke through Hosea, the LORD said to Hosea, "Go, take to yourself a wife of whoredom and have children of whoredom, for the land commits great whoredom by forsaking the LORD."
>
> —Hosea 1:2

The picture is this. Late Old Testament Israel had amassed a long history of synthesizing idol worship into their prescribed worship of God. In God's eyes, who viewed his relationship with his people as a marriage, this disloyalty was the same as adultery. The prophetic writings from the eighth- to the sixth-century BC are full of this adultery/apostasy theme. God, like a jilted husband, became furious with jealousy.

When Hosea grew to adulthood in the mid-eighth-century BC, the LORD called him to take his prophetic message to Israel. His call included showing them God's message symbolically. Hosea's marriage to a prostitute, with all the fallout that would come from her unfaithfulness, became a real-life drama for the people to watch. The grief that Hosea experienced with his wife was the same as what God had experienced with his people.

Hosea's story could have been a candidate for a television drama. Here is how it plays out. He chooses a woman named Gomer, the daughter of Diblaim (Hos. 1:3). After the marriage, they have a son together, but after all, she is a prostitute. Where the text is clear about their first child, "She conceived and bore *him* a son" (Hos. 1:3-4), it is ambiguous about the next two births. "She conceived again and bore a daughter" (Hos. 1:6), whom Hosea symbolically names No-Mercy. Then, "When she had weaned No Mercy, she conceived and bore a son" (Hos. 1:8). Probably she conceived both children by other men.

Gomer's unfaithfulness escalates when she leaves Hosea to live with someone else. When she and her new boyfriend run out of money for food, Hosea delivers groceries, only to have the man slam the door in his face and claim that he had bought them (Hos. 2:7-8). The downward spiral continues until Gomer hits bottom and lands on the auction block as a slave. Hosea's final act of sacrificial love came when he buys her out of slavery and takes her again as his wife (Hos. 3:1-3).

For the pastor-counselor, Hosea's act of love became a test case. If

Hosea could forgive his unfaithful wife, then his counselee's sole duty was to follow his example and forgive the man who had molested her.

The problem with this kind of comparison becomes apparent when we examine it carefully. In forcing two different situations together, the counselor misrepresented both the nature and the intent of the book. The two actions had nothing to do with each other.

Hosea's marriage to Gomer constituted a deliberate choice as an adult, in obedience to God's command. The marriage became an object lesson so that the people could see God's anguish over what they had done. Hosea's consent to take Gomer as his wife had nothing to do with involuntary childhood sexual violation.

Nor was the book of Hosea meant to be a metaphor for off-the-charts forgiveness. The book never says, "Go and do likewise." In using the book against his counselee, the counselor minimized her pain and robbed her of any voice.

Reasserting the Language of Grief

In the case above, wrong counsel pushed a wounded victim into deeper pain through a wholly unbiblical set of expectations. Instead of healing, it only hurt her even more deeply. Here are five reasons why forgive-and-forget teaching shows a lack of compassion toward victims and fails as a biblical approach.

First, when counsel requires forgiveness as the only legitimate response to being wronged, it consigns the victim's pain to irrelevance. It erases her significance as a person and takes away her right to mourn her losses. We never see this demand in the psalms of lament. Instead, we see what Old Testament scholar Walter Brueggemann calls the "language of grief."[59] The language is a loud and personal protest against the situation. Westermann describes it this way:

> The laments almost always dwelt on the shame which the isolation of grief brought with it. Suffering was consistently viewed in its social aspects. Everyone forsook the sufferer; they fled from him as from a leper; they pointed their fingers at him and said that God had forsaken him. This was the depth of suffering and the real sharpness of the trial.[60]

What was true during biblical times remains true today. Those who have been wronged can suffer twice—once for the wrong itself, and a second time when they find they cannot meet the unrealistic demands of "Forgive and forget." In truth, the Bible never calls us to set aside our need to grieve our injustices.

Second, the forgive-and-forget approach demands compassion from the victim. The person becomes a project. The emphasis moves from addressing the offense to correcting the victim's attitude toward the perpetrator. If the victim cannot make a direct move to forgiveness, then the project is declared unfinished.

Third, once the victim's pain is said to be irrelevant, the victim finds him- or herself called to dismiss the wrong. This forces the victim into one of two impossible choices. Either he must pretend to forgive while the injustice remains unresolved, or he begins to suffer as a guilty party for refusing to forgive. Often other people's testimonies of forgiveness become leverage against the victim. "If this person exercised forgiveness, then you should too." The victim is disallowed even the simple desire to see justice.

Fourth, when the focus rejects the need for justice and demands instant forgiveness instead, the person who committed the abuse drops out of the picture. Given the moral gyrations involved in rewriting the requirements for forgiveness, this outcome is only logical. When the "main" issue becomes forgiveness, both the victim's pain and the act that caused it cease to matter. And when we neglect the victim, the perpetrator slips into the background. Justice ceases to be the issue. For this reason, many innocent people suffer silently under the self-dismissive label of "victimless crimes."

Fifth, hasty forgiveness creates an atmosphere that diminishes the meaning of forgiveness itself. If forgiveness becomes only an expectation, then it loses the grace that was supposed to propel it. The end is anything but beautiful in the biblical sense.

> We become the good-humor men and women, for who among us does not want to rush in and smooth things out, to reassure, to cover the grief?...In a hospital room we want it to be cheery, and in a broken marriage we want to imagine it will be all right. We bring the lewd promise of immortality everywhere, which is not a promise but only a denial of what history brings and what we are indeed experiencing. In the Christian tradition...we are tempted to

legitimate the denial by offering crossless good news and
a future well-being without a present anguish.[61]

Direct-to-forgiveness thinking forces the wronged individual to go through the motions of forgiveness without allowing the injured person to process the wrong done. I believe direct-to-forgiveness teaching has become an act of New Testament legalism.

Psalm 109 and the Litany of Cursing

Biblical forgiveness recognizes the cost of the sin and refuses to minimize it for the sake of a quick dismissal. True biblical forgiveness offers pardon as an act of grace. The Psalms, in particular, give us a healthier and more natural response to personal injury. The cursing psalms do what the title implies. They call upon God to judge the ones who violated the writers. When we take the time to examine them, we find that they allow us to process our emotions in a way that permits us to pass the issue to God.

Psalm 109 is an example of the cursing psalms. This psalm, written by David, is dedicated "To the Choirmaster," making it part of the Old Testament worship hymnody. We can outline the psalm as follows:

A. David's plea for God to intervene against his detractors (verses 1-5)
B. The cursing section, (verses 5-20)
   1. Curses called down, (verses 6-15)
   2. The theology behind the curses, (verses 16-20)
C. The shift from anger to trust, (verses 21-31)
   1. David's plea for God's *hesed*, (verses 21-26)
   2. Confidence that God will vindicate himself, (verses 27-31)

Part A: David's Plea to God to Intervene against his Detractors, (verses 1-4)

In the first five verses, David issues his complaint. An unidentified group has attacked him verbally. At first, this statement may sound lightweight. Seriously, words? We all know the playground ditty, "Sticks and stones may break my bones, but words can never hurt me." In real life, however, the ditty holds no more substance than a bucket of air. Broken bones heal.

The wounds that arise from words can fester for a lifetime. When a boy or girl recites the ditty, often with a quavering voice, we know the words have done their job already. The Psalm begins,

> Be not silent, O God of my praise!
>> For wicked and deceitful mouths are opened against me,
>> speaking against me with lying tongues.
> They encircle me with words of hate,
>> and attack me without cause.
> In return for my love they accuse me,
>> but I give myself to prayer.

> Psalm 109:1-4

The opening mentions the three most important characters in the lament—God, David, and his enemies. In turn, it builds a catalog of the way each uses words:

- A plea to God to speak: Be not *silent* (verse 1)
- David's speech: O God of my *praise* (verse 1)
- David's accusers' speech:
  - Wicked and deceitful *mouths opened* against me (verse 2)
  - *Speaking* against me with *lying tongues* (verse 2)
  - *Words of hate* (verse 4)
  - They *accuse* (verse 4)
- David's self-discipline: I give myself to *prayer* (verse 4)

David's prayer is to the God of his praise, begging him to break his silence. It is purposeful speech. By contrast, the entire repertoire of his enemies consists of abusive language—deceitful mouths, lying tongues, words of hate, and accusations.

Verse 5 summarizes the situation and gives us a glimpse into its dynamics.

> So they reward me evil for good,
>> and hatred for my love.

> —Psalm 109:5

David has shown mercy towards his former friends, but they have returned hatred. Their behavior is unthinkable for David because the men for whom he cared have taken something precious and have returned slander.

David's Personal Enemy, (verses 6-15)

An important change occurs in the middle section of the psalm. The pronouns move from "they" and "them" to "he" and "him." An individual lies behind the group, and David now turns his sights toward him.

> Appoint a wicked man against *him*;
>> let an accuser stand at *his* right hand.
> When *he* is tried, let *him* come forth guilty;
>> let *his* prayer be counted as sin!

—Psalm 109:6-7

Prayer reenters the picture here in a particularly ironic way. In the introduction, David wrote, "But I am in prayer." Hebrew poetry is brief in its use of language, but this line is especially sparse. The literal translation of this line is, "But I [am] prayer." The wording shows David's close connection to his God.

The irony comes with the mention of his adversary's prayer, which David calls for God to count as sin (verse 7). Notice the irony. The fact that his enemy practices prayer shows us that he shares David's belief system, at least on the surface. David's enemy is more than an anonymous opponent. He is a man who had common ties with David within his faith circle, who now has turned against him.

Prayer and Cursing

Everything that David says in the psalm, including the cursing section, is a reflection of the statement in verse 4, "I give myself to prayer." In this case, however, prayer looks nothing like bleached white flour. "Nice" words are absent when David addresses the LORD. His personal feelings toward the man, his sense of betrayal, his anger, his desire to see the man pay for what he has done—all these appear in the cursing section. The realities we have covered in the opening chapters shape David's prayer. He recognizes that God is both powerful enough to deal with the evil and loving enough to care about his plight. His prayer is for the LORD to bring justice in majesty.

This fact does not leave David free to carry on in unbridled rage, however. When we enter into the middle of the psalm, we need to be clear about its boundaries. Here are some of David's liberties and restrictions in this psalm.

Liberties

- David has the right to tell God how his accuser has wounded him.
- He has the liberty to pray against his accuser.
- He is allowed to call for appropriate punishment against his accuser.
- He can call on God to act in majesty in his ministry of justice.
- He has the liberty to be satisfied when God acts.
- He has the right to trust God to work on his behalf.

Restrictions

- He does not have the liberty to take matters into his hands.
- He does not have the liberty to exceed the speech boundaries that God has set.
- He does not have the liberty to become gleeful or self-satisfied when God acts.
- He does not have the liberty to make personal boasts over his accuser when God brings justice.
- He does not have the liberty to make unreasonable demands to God concerning his accuser.

These rights and restrictions define the imprecatory psalms. David has a broad playing field, and he covers every square inch of it in his prayer. At the same time, he is equally aware of the boundaries. The emotion in the Psalms is never raw. It grows out of the way we listen to God.

One of the things David is allowed to do is to call for retribution or punishment that reflects the iniquities committed. David hints at this kind of punishment in verses 6-7. A full-blown call for retribution will begin in verse 17, but David anticipates it here. Where David recalled wickedness, lying tongues, and false accusations, he calls for God to send a wicked man to stand against the individual (verse 6).

Justice, Mercy, and the Call for God to Act

We do not know when, how, or why the events occurred. We can assume that the actions of the individual had become dangerous and apparently were severe enough to threaten David's family. The section bounded by verses 6-15 calls for several curses, and they follow a clear progression. David calls for:

- A wicked and false accuser to attach himself to the enemy (verse 6).
- His enemy's guilt to be secured and his prayer to become sin (verse 7).
- His days to become numbered and his office to revert to another man (verse 8).[62]
- The accuser's ultimate death (verse 9).
- His children to become unable to find gainful employment, (verses 10-12).
- His family to come to extinction by the second generation, (verse 13).
- The enemy's fathers' collective iniquity to work against him, (verse 14).
- The man and his family's memory to perish from the earth, (verse 15).

On the surface, Psalm 109 appears to fly in the face of New Testament teaching on forgiveness. When we see the kind of prayer in this Psalm, we assume it must belong to the angry God in the Old Testament, as opposed to the forgiving God of the New Testament. We forget that the same God rules over all of history. The God who forgives is the same God who brings evil men and women to justice.

Can we then reconcile the two viewpoints? I believe we can, provided we understand the Bible's use of cursing in the Psalms along in light of Jesus' teaching on forgiveness. Let us look at Jesus' teaching first.

Centuries after David, Peter asks the question, "Lord, how often will my brother sin against me, and I forgive him? As many as seven times?"

(Matthew 18:21). Jesus' answer shatters the notion. "I do not say to you seven times, but seventy times seven" (Matthew 18:22). In other words, if you have to count, you have missed the point of forgiveness.

However, Jesus never intends for forgiveness to ignore the infraction. The parable he uses to illustrate the principle shows this. A king's servant had accrued a debt of ten thousand talents, equivalent to well over a million dollars. Because of the debt, the king ordered the servant, his family, and his possessions to help pay the collection fee. The entire family would become slaves.

The man, left without any other recourse, makes an egregious plea. "Have patience with me, and I will pay you everything" (Matthew 18:26). The promise is as absurd as it is desperate. But the king's response is even more outrageous. *"And out of pity for him,* the master of that servant released him and forgave him the debt" (Matthew 18:27, emphasis added). Jesus has shown forgiveness in all its glory.

The story takes an ironic turn, however. The servant turns around and accosts one of his fellow servants, demanding that he pay him back a hundred denarii debt, about four month's wages for the average worker (Matthew 18:28). The fellow servant's reply is eerily similar to the first servant. "Have patience with me, and I will repay you" (Matthew 18:30). Unlike the first servant's request, his friend's request is reasonable. But the first servant refuses to listen and threatens his fellow servant.

The other servants see what has transpired and tell the king. The king, in turn, summons the first servant to declare justice. In Jesus' words, *"And in anger* his master delivered him to the jailers, until he should pay all his debt" (Matthew 18:34). The next verse reads, *"So also* my heavenly Father will do to every one of you, if you do not forgive your brother from your heart" (Matthew 18:35).

At first, this statement appears to contradict Psalm 109, but a closer examination reveals otherwise. In the parable, the king's act of forgiveness (and by implication, the heavenly Father's) is an act of grace. As sovereign King, God is free to forgive, and he is also free to condemn.

Jesus extends the requirement for forgiveness to his followers *to the degree that they seek the Father's mercy.* For this reason, when the servant in the parable denies mercy to his fellow servant, he breaks his connection to forgiveness with his master. As a result, the king shifts his stance toward the servant from grace to justice. He applies the same standard to the servant with the greater debt as that servant forced on his fellow.

Jesus has shown a perfect balance between forgiveness and justice. When we extend this thinking to Psalm 109, we see David calling on the LORD to administer justice to one who has done to David what the servant in Jesus' parable did to his friend. David's enemy, one who makes pretense to pray, acts only with treachery toward David. He shows neither remorse nor desire for mercy. He has no desire to *be* forgiven. These factors become the basis for David's plea to God to bring justice. The principle becomes even more evident when David enters into the theology of God's justice and mercy.

The Theology behind the Curse

The focal point for the justice issue appears in verses 14-15.

> May the iniquity of his fathers be remembered before
>   the LORD,
>   and let not the sin of his mother be blotted out!
> Let them be before the LORD continually,
>   that he may cut off the memory of them from the earth!
>
> —Psalm 109:14-15

Upon first reading, David's plea for justice appears to run roughshod over the boundaries discussed above. Where does he find justification to call a curse to descend on the man's entire family?

The theological underpinning for this psalm occurs in Exodus 34, when Moses is on the mountain to receive the Ten Commandments and asks the LORD to show his glory. The complete declaration bears repeating here. The first portion proclaims God's mercy:

> The LORD descended in the cloud and stood with him there, and proclaimed the name of the LORD. The LORD passed before him and proclaimed, "The LORD, the LORD, a God merciful and gracious, slow to anger, and abounding in steadfast love and faithfulness, keeping steadfast love for thousands, forgiving iniquity and transgression and sin...
>
> —Exodus 34:5-7a

These words show the Old Testament God to be as gracious as the New Testament God. He is a God who forgives. But his graciousness is balanced by justice. God's declaration to Moses concludes,

> ...but who will by no means clear the guilty, *visiting the iniquity of the fathers on the children and the children's children, to the third and the fourth generation."*

—Exodus 34: 7b, emphasis added

We cannot understand the relationship between justice and mercy until we see how the two qualities relate to each other. Yes, God acts in grace, and sometimes his actions are inexplicable. But as we saw in the commentary on Job and Psalm 9/10, God's self-imposed mission is to act in justice. It is the way he demonstrates his majesty.

When David calls for the LORD to drive his enemy's family into extinction by the second generation, he speaks according to this declaration from Exodus. For those who are willing to seek God's compassion, the LORD is full of mercy, slow to anger, gracious, full of steadfast love, and filled with a spirit of forgiveness. Those who resist God's steadfast love, as this man has, can expect justice as the natural recourse from God. God is as praiseworthy when he exercises justice as he is when he acts in mercy.

Retribution, the "Just" Justice

In Psalm 109:16-20 David expresses his anger in the form of retributive curses. His words form an explicit call for justice.

- David's enemy rejected kindness and pursued the poor and needy. He put the broken hearted to death. He practiced cursing, so let curses come upon him, (verses 16-17a).
- He rejected blessing. Therefore let blessing be far from him, (verse 17b).
- He wore the curse like a cloak. In retribution, let curses against him soak into his body like water, like oil into his bones, like a garment wrapped around him, and like a belt, (verses 18-19).

Every curse resides within the boundaries that Exodus declares. David describes retributive justice in terms that reflect what his enemy has done. He calls for the man's cursing to come back on him. He calls for his enemy's refusal to bless to be an occasion for God to withhold blessing. If his enemy is so fascinated by cursing, then let the curse saturate his body.

The section ends with the summary statement that reverts to the plural, "my accusers." This break not only marks David's end to his speech against his personal enemy. It also marks the end of the cursing section of the psalm. Now he is ready to give the matter to the LORD.

> May this be the reward of my accusers from the LORD,
> of those who speak evil against my life!

> —Psalm 109:20

David's Shift to Petition and Praise

The final section begins with the *vav*-adversative. Here the theme shifts the focus from David's enemy to his God. *"But you,* O God my Lord, / deal on my behalf for your name's sake; / because your steadfast love is good, deliver me!" (verse 21). David expands the petition by turning his language toward himself. Here are the terms that he uses to describe himself as a petitioner in this section.

- I am poor and needy, (verse 22a)
- My heart is stricken, (verse 22b)
- I am gone like a shadow, (verse 23a)
- I am shaken off like a locust, (verse 23b)
- My knees are weak through, fasting (verse 24a)
- My body has become gaunt, (verse 24b)
- I am an object of scorn to my accusers, (verse 25a)

These are not pictures of David feeling sorry for himself. Instead, they mark the language of subjection to his God. They expand David's declaration in verse 4, "But I give myself to prayer" (ESV).

In verses 21 and 26, David uses the Hebrew word, *hesed,* signifying the LORD's steadfast, enduring love. The two instances of the term occur at the beginning and the end of this section. The bulleted list of self-descriptions above falls between these two occurrences of the word. Every plea appeals to God's *hesed*, or his abounding kindness to those who suffer.

For the psalm writers, biblical justice does not mean that God seeks to prevent bad things from happening to good people. It says that God comes to the aid of the helpless who suffer unjustly, the ones who call to the LORD in genuine faith.

When David builds his personal character portrait, he does not paint himself as a good man who suffers unjustly. He characterizes himself as humble (meaning subordinate to God), poor, and needy. These characteristics stand in contrast to his accusers, who are self-important, arrogant, and proud. David places himself in subjection to God while his accusers flaunt themselves.

A Plea for God to Vindicate Himself

We come to the conclusion of the psalm, where the issue shifts from David's problem to his problem-solving God. As he makes a second plea for God to demonstrate his *hesed,* his focus moves to the way he wishes the LORD to manifest himself through justice.

> Help me, O LORD my God!
>> Save me according to your steadfast love (*hesed*)!
> Let them know that this is your hand;
>> you, O LORD have done it!
> Let them curse, but you will bless!
>> They arise and are put to shame, but your servant will be glad!
> May my accusers be clothed with dishonor;
>> may they be wrapped in their own shame as in a cloak!

> —Psalm 109:26-29

These lines are confident rather than desperate. David begins to rest in the assurance that the LORD will vindicate his cause. The transformation from desperation to faith is as dramatic as any in the psalms of lament. We continue to see David's pain, but we also witness God's light breaking through his grief.

The change is progressive. As God's light shines ever more brightly, David can look forward to the praise he will give after his mourning is taken away. The verses above comprise the next-to-last section of the psalm, and they mark David's transition. The section begins with pleas for rescue: "Help me...Save me...Let them know that this is in your hand..." (verses 26-27).

Following that, David begins to operate in the realm of certainty: "... but you will bless! They...are put to shame, but your servant will be glad!" (verses 28).

The section ends with a final call for his accusers' downfall, a call which bears a close resemblance to his curse on the ringleader. Like his earlier plea against the ringleader, David calls for the group to be "clothed with dishonor" and "wrapped in their own shame" (verse 29). Here, though, his words lack the edge that they had before. The call now is more of a statement of faith than of cursing. His words become a confession of faith. The LORD is going to resolve the issue.

David knows that God will bless and that God's very blessing will become the cause for his accusers' dishonor and shame. The boundaries he has set for himself have kept him from falling into a wish for personal vengeance. His hope is for vindication.

The Vow of Praise

The psalm ends in anticipation of the joy that will come. God *will* intercede on David's behalf, and he *will* vindicate him.

> With my mouth I will give great thanks to the LORD:
>   I will praise him in the midst of the throng.
> For he stands at the right hand of the needy,
>   to save him from those who condemn his soul to death.

> —Psalm 109:30-31

Here are a few observations on the verses above:

- The vow of praise always points back to the particular issue for which the psalmist prayed—in this case, vindication.
- Praise is a testimony stated out loud, "with my mouth." It is not just a privately held feeling of gratitude.
- Praise will be public, "in the midst of the throng."
- Praise recognizes what God does. In this psalm, "He stands at the right hand of the needy...."
- Praise is God-directed, as a confession of faith. The person coming with praise does not announce, "This is what happened." Instead, he or she says, "This is what God has done for me." Westermann describes praise this way: "God has intervened; he has saved. This, however, is never said as a statement of fact, but always as a confession. That is to say, the one who utters this sentence backs it up with his own existence; he is committed to the fact that this has happened to him."[63]

The transformative character of prayer spoken in honesty now becomes evident. David's plea before the LORD is a full confession of his pain and his desire to see justice performed. But beyond that, it is a testimony to his freedom to mourn. If David matters to God, then his betrayal also matters to God. He has the right to address it out loud.

Here is where the transformation from cursing to forgiveness begins. When we express our desperation by asking God to act in justice, grace rises out of our plea in a natural fashion. Samuel Terrien writes, "Invoking salvation and receiving it as a gift from heaven, the psalmist discerns that this will become the preaching of a 'gospel'; the Good News or 'God's spell': God loves man."[64]

"Go to Forgiveness. You May Pass Go and You May Collect $200"

At first, the connection between this psalm and forgiveness appears to be as distant as Hawaii is from California. We might as well try to row to the islands as to make the journey from cursing to forgiveness. When we understand the curse as a plea for justice, its connection to forgiveness falls into place.

What is forgiveness, then? How do we describe it in Bible-honoring terms?

In broad brushstrokes, forgiveness is a conscious choice to acknowledge God's just intervention on our behalf and to refrain from counting people's sins against them. It is a declaration that says, "I release you from what you did because I have given that issue to God." The operating phrase, "I release you," has substance because it reflects our choice to operate in grace rather than denial. It never means, "Aw, it doesn't matter."

The psalm avoids a straight-line path to forgiveness. It moves through honest mourning, anger, desire for justice, and finally resolution. The short Hebrew line in verse 4—literally, "But I am prayer"—encompasses all those emotions. Everything in this psalm shows prayer in agony. Through the course of the psalm, David has made his appeal to God. He has unloaded his thoughts. He has fasted to the point of physical deprivation. Now, he can place his situation in God's hands.

From here, the movement to genuine forgiveness falls within walking distance. Forgiveness becomes an acknowledgment of joy that grows out of praise, rather than a legal issue. In effect, the plea to God signs off on the issue. It allows God—who calls for prayer from his saints—to bring justice as he desires. God is free to act in judgment or mercy. Should he choose to do so, he can call David's enemy to repentance. And since our prayer has placed the whole issue in God's hands, the petitioner will be able to rejoice if God chooses to grant grace.

The first time I taught this psalm in a group setting, an unexpected phenomenon occurred. Toward the end of the discussion, one of the members began to talk about the possibility of speaking the salvation message to a person like the one David described in this psalm. The subject arose naturally, without any sense of imposed spirituality. It happened when we understood the need for our emotions to complete their journeys. When we lay our anger, hurt, and resentment before the Lord, we cannot help but think like the Lord. That includes showing mercy and forgiveness.

Journal Entry

The imprecatory psalms are all about prayer before God. They are about honesty, self-control, and submission. Perhaps someone has wronged you in a serious way, and you have been unable to deal with the issue. The exercise below calls you to write a lament. Your lament will allow you to walk through your pain, to address the way that the person has hurt you, to call on God to perform justice, and then to leave the issue in God's hands. God will work. He declared, "Vengeance is mine, and recompense....For the Lord will vindicate his people and have compassion on his servants..." (Deuteronomy 32:35, 36; the Apostle Paul quotes this verse in Romans 12:19).

The outline for the lament follows Psalm 109. Your lament will be a private issue between you and God. Write the prayer on a medium that you can discard. When you are through, take your prayer to an appropriate place, pray over it, and release it to God. Then destroy your medium as a gesture of release.

What is your plea to God, and why do you make it (verses 1-2)? _____

_____

_____

_____

What has the person done to you, (verses 3-5)? _____

_____

_____

_____

How do you want to see God to carry out justice (not personal vengeance) toward the person, (verses 6-15)? _____

_____

_____

_____

What summary statement can you make concerning the way the person violated God's principles, (verses 16-20)? _____

_____

_____

_____

What is your emotional position before God as you write this lament, and why do you want the Lord to act on your behalf, (verses 21-25)? _____

_____

_____

_____

Since this lament is an exercise in personal faith, how do you intend to give this burden to the Lord? What do you want the Lord to do in order to make you glad, (verses 26-29)? _____

_____

_____

_____

When the time comes to give public testimony on what God's intervention has accomplished (see Chapter 11 on Psalm 116), how will you give public praise to him for what he has done? _____

_____

_____

_____

A final note: You may find that after you have gone through this material, you still find yourself unable to forgive. Forgiveness, particularly for deep wounds, does not come easily. If you need to continue to take the issue to God in prayer, do so. Repeat the process until the Lord grants you genuine forgiveness. You will discover the Lord's peace.

CHAPTER 11

Psalm 116

From Mourning to Praise

Mourning turns to songs of praise[65]

Recognizing the Light

Just as each of the Psalms highlights a different place along the spectrum of mourning to praise, deliverance will come to mean something unique to each of us.

- For some, it will mean nothing less than complete release from our suffering, shame, or fear.
- For others, it will come to mean acceptance of personal losses.
- Still, others may discover an ability to understand their circumstances as a prelude to a greater call.
- Some will experience forgiveness and reconciliation.
- Others will come to realize acceptance with God when human forgiveness is impossible.
- In every case, deliverance will indicate a deeper personal intimacy with God.

I stress these examples because of the human tendency to project our present circumstances into our personal futures. When everything is going well, we want to believe the time to come will be equally successful. Likewise, when difficulty rolls on endlessly, we often fall into a victim mentality where we define the remainder of our lives by our negative circumstances. Extended periods of time without hope cast a low cloud deck over our lives, and this, in turn, begins to lead to cynicism. We can become blinded to deliverance and may miss it when it comes. For that reason, we need to keep our covenant relationship with the Lord in clear focus. God does not leave the believer without hope. The Psalms always look toward praise.

The Vow of Praise Revisited

Sometimes circumstances call us to practice recognition as an act of discipline. Such was the case in 2 Chronicles 20, for example, when Moabite and Ammonite armies stood against the country of Judah during King Jehoshaphat's reign. From a human standpoint, the nation would lose. Jehoshaphat's plea to the LORD ended with the words, "We are powerless against this great horde that is coming against us. We do not know what to do, but our eyes are on you" (2 Chr. 20:12).

God honored his confession. When Jehoshaphat prayed, the Spirit of the LORD came upon a Levite named Jehaziel, who prophesied that the LORD would deliver the nation without a fight. Jehoshaphat believed the promise, and the next morning appointed singers to walk ahead of the armies. In honor of God's promise to deliver, the people determined to praise the LORD beforehand for the victory he had promised. When they came to the battlefield, they found only carnage, and they realized that the LORD had turned the invading armies against each other. The invaders all died in confusion.

Examples this dramatic are rare. God does not expect us to achieve joy by practicing all praise all the time because life does not allow celebration all the time. By itself, praise does not guarantee that God will bring deliverance. In Jehoshaphat's case, liberation did not emerge from praise. The nation worshiped because the LORD had promised to deliver them.

As Chapter 4 pointed out, praise and lament mark the two poles of spiritual experience, and neither can exist alone. Praise draws its force from joy, and joy emerges in deliverance, in the assurance that salvation will come, or in gratitude for God's blessings. Lament cries out from the opposite pole as it calls for God to deliver. The psalmists understood this. Their laments anchored themselves in the bedrock conviction that God was big enough to change history. As the hymn writer Edward Mote wrote, "When darkness veils his lovely face, I rest on his unchanging grace."[66]

The sentiment is fine in theory, but what happens when darkness becomes claustrophobic and even a step in faith can send us hurtling? How do we find our way back from mourning to praise when lament is all we know?

Planting Direction Markers to Praise

For the psalmists, God's unchanging grace took the form of *hesed*, or his everlasting and indestructible covenant kindness. But mere belief in God's goodness was not enough. They also needed a place to plant it. The vow of praise became their survey marker, an objective reference point outside themselves where they could pin their hope. *When*—not if—the LORD answered, they would respond in public praise.

The vow of praise performed at least three functions for the petitioner. First, it kept the petitioner consciously focused on the deliverance he or she sought. Second, it required the person to place his trust in the God who would save. Third, it disciplined him to prepare a response when God delivered. Often the psalmists declared their vows out loud, as they did in these laments:

> The LORD judges the peoples;
>> judge me, O LORD, according to my righteousness
>> and according to the integrity that is in me....
> *I will give to the LORD thanks* [lit. I will laud the
>> LORD] due to his righteousness,
>> *and I will sing praise* to the name of the Most High.
>
> —Psalm 7:8, 17, emphasis added

> Deliver my soul from the sword,
>> my precious life from the power of the dog!
>> Save me from the mouth of the Lion!
> You have rescued me from the horns of the wild oxen!
> *I will tell of your name to my brothers,*
>> *in the midst of the congregation I will praise you...*
>
> —Psalm 22:20-22, emphasis added

> Attend to my cry,
>> for I am brought very low!
> Deliver me from my persecutors,
>> for they are too strong for me!
> Bring me out of prison,
>> *that I may give thanks to [lit. laud] your name...*

—Psalm 142:6-7a, emphasis added

The vow separates the petitioners from their problem and redirects their focus toward the Lord. It is one of the most important strategies that the psalmists employ to maintain their focus God's ability to deliver.

Psalm 116: A Vow Observed

Psalm 116 is a hymn of praise to God for having rescued the psalmist. In it, the writer considers how he will fulfill his vow of praise. God has delivered the writer, and now he prepares to celebrate his release from the sorrow that had been his living death. The Psalm is a portrait of the relief that arises after deliverance has taken place. Having been freed from extreme difficulty, the psalmist prepares to celebrate God's victory. Thematically, the psalm divides into two broad sections:

Part 1: Mapping the journey from mourning to praise (verses 1-11)

Part 2: Meditation on the fulfillment of the vow (verses 12-19)

Part I: Mapping the Journey from Mourning to Praise, (verses 1-11)

When the psalmist describes his deliverance from torment (verses 1-11), his relief is palpable. He begins,

> I love the LORD, because he has heard
>> my voice and my pleas for mercy.
> Because he inclined his ear to me,
>> therefore I will call on him as long as I live.

—Psalm 116:1-2

God has made good on his covenant promise, and the psalmist is ready to devote the rest of his life to the kind of trust that remembers God as a covenant keeper. That sort of confidence builds on the memory of the vow made when the psalmist was in crisis. Since God has rescued him from imminent death, the most logical thing he can do is to maintain his trust in him.

The reason for his joy appears in the next two verses. The threat that had terrified him has vanished.

> The snares of death encompassed me,
>> the pangs of Sheol laid hold on me;
>> I suffered distress and anguish.
> Then I called on the name of the LORD:
>> "O LORD, I pray, deliver my soul!"

—Psalm 116:3-4

The next three verses develop a section of descriptive praise that speaks about God's work in general terms. At their conclusion, the writer celebrates his deliverance.

> Gracious is the LORD, and righteous;
>> our God is merciful.
> The LORD preserves the simple [i.e. those who are open
>> to his instruction];
>> when I was brought low, he saved me.
> Return, O my soul, to your rest;
>> for the LORD has dealt bountifully with you.

—Psalm 116:5-7

In contrast to the psalms of lament, which often express the psalmists' difficulties in detail, this psalm mentions the darker times only briefly. The time to rehearse the challenges has passed. Now, the writer can call the people together to celebrate the LORD's act of deliverance.[67] The good, rather than the evil, has become the focal point.

Verses 8-9 form a short section of thanksgiving, followed by a brief recollection of the difficulty that caused his pain in the first place.

143

> For you have delivered my soul from death,
>> my eyes from tears;
>> my feet from stumbling.
> I will walk before the LORD in the land of the living.
> I believed, even when I spoke,
>> "I am greatly afflicted!"[68]
> I said in my alarm,
>> "All mankind are liars!"

—Psalm 116:8-11

These words express a sense of wonder at the psalmist's deliverance. They sound almost breathless as he tries to comprehend the unfathomable. "I'm free." His words are less a cry for help as an expression of awe. This realization leads naturally to the question that dominates the latter part of the psalm.

Part 2: Meditation on the Fulfillment of a Vow, (verses 12-19)

Part II changes the writer's focus from the past to the future. Now that the LORD has delivered him, how will he fulfill his vow?

> What shall I render to the LORD
>> for all his benefits to me?
> I will lift up the cup of salvation
>> and call on the name of the LORD,
> I will pay my vows to the LORD
>> in the presence of all his people.

—Psalm 116:12-14

In the original language, the first person ("I") occurs five times in this section of the psalm, and yet the meditation is selfless. The word order in the poetry makes this even more apparent. Here is a literal translation that follows the word order in the three verses, with the emphasized phrases appearing in boldface type.

12. What shall I return to the LORD
    for all his benefits to me?
13. **The cup of salvation** I will bring,
    and **to the name of the LORD** I will call.
14. **My vows to the LORD** I will complete,
    before, I pray, all the people.

The emphasis here focuses on the manner in which the writer's actions will bring glory to the LORD for his work on his behalf. The words, "I pray" (verse 14), are awkward in English and do not appear in modern Bibles. Nonetheless, they serve to demonstrate the psalmist's humility before the LORD. Even his vow of praise becomes a prayer to honor God in the completion of his vows.

God has entered into history, not because he needs to be a hero, but because he has committed himself to demonstrating justice in an unjust world. His self-appointed task is to come to the aid of his people. He has established a covenant relationship with them in which he promises to be their deliverer. In our relationship with God, he is always the giver, and we are always the receivers.

The psalmist recognizes God's sovereign rank over his people. Therefore, when he asks, "What shall I render to the LORD," his question points to worship. His question means, "How can I respond appropriately to acknowledge everything God has done for me?" The answer becomes clear: "I will pay my vows to the LORD / in the presence of all his people" (verse 14). What better act can we perform than to laud God's name publically so that his praise becomes widespread?[69] We are created to experience awe, and wonder leads directly to praise. Mowinckel writes,

> The core of the hymn of praise is the consciousness of the poet and congregation that they are standing face to face with the Lord himself, meeting the almighty, holy and merciful God in his place, and worshipping him with praise and adoration. He is in their midst, and they are his chosen people, who owe him everything. Therefore they now meet him, with awe and trembling because he is the Holy One, but also with a sure trust, love, jubilation and overflowing enthusiasm, while remembering all the great and glorious things that he has done.[70]

Death: A Terror to dread or a Blessing to Anticipate?

Verses 15-17 continue the line of thought begun in verses 12-14.

> Precious in the sight of the LORD
> is the death of his saints.
> O LORD, I am your servant;
> I am your servant, the son of your maidservant.
> You have loosed my bonds.
> I will offer to you the sacrifice of thanksgiving
> and call on the name of the LORD.

—Psalm 116:16-17

The term "saints" in the second line does not refer to a specially recognized class of holy people. It is the word the Bible uses for all who belong to God. Different versions have rendered the term as "godly ones" or "holy ones." Those who belong to God possess a close and precious relationship to their God when they die.

The statement regarding the death of the saints has proven to be difficult for commentators because it appears to be so out of place in this psalm. On the surface, the statement seems to drop out of the sky. Why does this interjection about death appear after the psalmist expresses his desire to make good on his vow of praise? Scholars' interpretations lean toward a view that recognizes the inevitability of mortality. Here is a typical example.

> The use of *yāqār* [be dignified, honorable, heavy, valuable]
> to describe the death of the LORD's *hesed* [beloved] ones
> indicates that God does not happily accept the death of any
> faithful one, but considers life the better alternative and
> counts each death as costly and *weighty.*[71]

While death is inevitable, that fact does not concern the psalmist in this part of the psalm. The writer expresses nothing about either anguish or the inevitability of death. I believe we can come to a better sense of resolution by observing the use of the word in context. The writer mentions death three times in this psalm, each in different circumstances. Viewed together, they appear to represent distinct landmarks in his personal journey from mourning to praise.

- **The danger of death during his torment:** "The snares of death encompassed me; / the pangs of Sheol laid hold of me" (verse 3)
- **Deliverance from death:** "For you have delivered my soul from death..." (verse 8)
- **Death as fulfillment:** "Precious in the sight of the LORD is the death of his saints" (verse 15)

In the first statement in verse 3, death remains a threat, placing the writer's covenant relationship with his God in danger. Should death overtake him before the LORD rescues him, he would depart from the world before God had brought resolution to his situation. Consequently, the writer would be unable to fulfill his vow to praise God for deliverance. This attitude toward death is typical in the Psalms. For the ancient Hebrews, normal life meant the ability to offer public praise to God for his acts of deliverance. Threats from the outside interrupted the people's ability to carry on normal worship, and death represented the final and absolute disruption from praise. At this stage, cessation of life would have destroyed the writer's relationship with his Deliverer prematurely.[72]

The second statement marks the writer's escape from the conflict that death represented in verse 3. The deliverance is threefold. "For you have delivered my soul from death, / my eyes from tears, / my feet from stumbling" (verse 8). The result is that "I will walk before the LORD / in the land of the living" (verse 9). The psalmist's walk represents the totality of a life in the LORD's presence and includes the fulfillment of his vow. The writer states his intent to fulfill the vow as a threefold declaration as well, phrasing it as a request before the LORD. Here again is the literal translation of verses 13-14:

> The cup of salvation I will bring,
>   and to the name of the LORD I will call.
> My vows to the LORD I will complete,
>   before, I pray, all the people.
>
> —Psalm 116:13-14

By the time we reach the third reference to death, everything that threatened the writer in verse 3 has vanished. His escape is complete. He is free to bring his offering, which he describes as "the cup of salvation." He will call on the name of the LORD and complete the vow he had made when he was in distress.

These facts suggest that the words, "Precious in the sight of the LORD is the death of his saints" (verse 15), indicate completeness. He is free to enter his final rest in fulfillment. The value of the saints' death in this context may signify the conclusion of a blessed life that would be impossible in his former terror. Having been freed from the earlier conflict, the psalmist can anticipate a peaceful death.

The Gospel of Luke records a similar self-assessment in Simeon's prophecy when he saw Jesus at his temple circumcision. According to Luke's Gospel, the Holy Spirit had revealed that Simeon "would not see death before he had seen the Lord's Christ" (Luke 2:26). When Mary and Joseph brought Jesus to the temple for his ritual circumcision, Simeon took the child in his arms and said,

> Lord, *now you are letting your servant depart in peace,*
>   according to your word;
> for my eyes have seen your salvation
>   that you have prepared in the presence of all peoples,
> a light for revelation to the Gentiles,
>   and for glory to your people Israel.
>
> —Luke 2:29-32, emphasis added

Like Simeon, the psalmist appears to express a sense of settledness. When the LORD fulfills his covenant promises, his saints can face death with confidence.

Paying the Vow

The psalm ends with the psalmist's final words of promise, the fulfillment of his pledge. Verses 17-19 describe the psalmist's preparation for the vow. The psalmist will bring a sacrifice to the LORD, and he will offer it at the temple in the presence of the people. These last lines return to a sense of wonder.

I will offer to you the sacrifice of thanksgiving
  and call on the name of the LORD.
I will pay my vows to the LORD
  in the presence of all his people,
In the courts of the house of the LORD,
  in your midst, O Jerusalem.
Praise the LORD!

—Psalm 116:17-19

Again, the author represents his intent with a triple declaration. Translated literally, *"I will offer* to you the sacrifice...*I will call* on the name...*I will pay* my vows...."

The Significance of a Vow

When God delivers and the time comes for the person to pay the vows he or she has made, what happens?

The occasion becomes a time of joy. The vow never leaves the petitioner with a lifetime of indentured service in return for the favor. After all, what could God demand from us that he does not already have? For that reason, the fulfillment section in the vow is an act of joy by which the petitioner invited the faithful to celebrate God's deliverance. It marks a time for celebration. God never intends to diminish the individual's joy with a lingering sense of debt.

The vow of praise is neither a bargaining chip for the petitioner to use to close a sale with God nor a tool for God to blackmail the person seeking his favor later. It is simply an affirmation of trust with expectation. "God will deliver, and I will take the news of his act to the people who matter to me."

In the Psalms, the vow always takes place under the anticipation of public praise. God delights in our joy. Like a child's mother or father, God delights to help us. Therefore, just as we have the right to mourn our difficulties, we have the equal right to celebrate our return to joy. Thanksgiving is an expression of our joy, and the vow of praise is simply an affirmation of our relationship with God. It is a promise to laud God, to depend on him, and to bring glory to him through praise.

Remaining Questions

A couple of explanatory questions remain. First, how exactly do we define "owing God"? To answer this question, we need to understand the two possible meanings of *owing*. One involves the anticipation of payback, often with interest. The obligation is never the intent with the Psalms. God is neither a bookie nor a lending institution. He does not keep score over our lives. If we owed him in that sense, no one would be solvent.

The other meaning reflects the recognition of a favor or act of kindness. Suppose a fireman carries an unconscious person from a burning building just before the building collapses. Later, when the fireman is honored for his act of heroism, the victim might come forward and tell the audience, "I owe this man my life." This use of *owing* has nothing to do with remuneration. It involves recognition. If we belong to God, he is our Father. The vow of praise is a promise based on gratitude and involves our intent to honor God for saving us. Asaph, whom we discussed earlier in this book, presents this sentiment in Psalm 50.

> Offer to God a sacrifice of thanksgiving,
>   and perform your vows to the Most High,
> and call upon me in the day of trouble;
>   I will deliver you, and you shall glorify me.
>
> —Psalm 50:14-15

The other question points to the nature of God's grace. Are we to approach God as though we have only a limited number of grace refills?

Absolutely not. God never places limits on grace. He never tells us we have reached our quota. When we find ourselves in difficulty again, we are to call upon him. The fact that we continue to trust him when the next crisis occurs signifies our continuing faith rather than its lack. We understand that he who delivered us in the past will continue to be faithful in the future. God wants us to keep coming back to him, which is what a good father would want from his children. When I was a young father, one of my chief joys was watching my three girls run to me whenever I came home from work. God takes pleasure in this kind of delight from us. When he walks in the door, he wants us to run toward him with our arms outstretched.

Journal Entry

Westermann writes, "The vow of praise...means in simple words that he will tell others what God has done for him."[73] How do you intend to tell others what God has done for you? Remember that you can do other activities beside verbal testimony. You can show your gratitude through art, music, acts of service to others, or any number of ways. _____

_____

_____

_____

PART 3

BUILDING A FOUNDATION
IN HOPE

CHAPTER 12

The New Testament Reality of Hope

I believe there is a meaning [in my chronic physical pain]. I know God loves me and cares for me and won't in the long run let me down. That's what gives me the hope to get up another day and face life's unpredictability. But I can't presume to know precisely what that meaning is. At least not yet.[74]

Introduction

A great deal of nineteenth- and early twentieth-century biblical teaching drew black-and-white divisions between historical periods in the Bible. Because of this, contemporary Christianity, in general, has fallen into the notion that the New Testament has made the Old Testament irrelevant. We often relegate the first three-quarters of the Bible to the status of the Obsolete Testament and let it go unnoticed. When we do such a thing, we rob ourselves. The Old Testament offers depth in worship that we cannot achieve by reading the New Testament alone.

However, we need to recognize that the New Testament does bring certain changes into the way we approach God. These changes do not take the form of replacement truth. Instead, they show God's grace to be something far greater than what the earlier saints understood.

Promises that Remain the Same

When we move from the Old Testament to the New, certain things remain unchanged. Here are some of the truths that endure throughout the Bible.

- God continues to love his people.
- God still answers prayer.
- God still enters into covenant relationship with his people. The words *Testament* and *Covenant* derive from the same biblical word. Our present day relationship with God is every bit as much a covenant relationship as the fellowship that the believers in the Old Testament enjoyed.
- People in the New Testament continue to offer laments and pleas to God. One example occurs in the early church at Jerusalem after the temple leaders forbade the apostles to preach Jesus as the Jewish Messiah (Acts 4:23-30). The church people cried out to the Lord in lament and asked him to give them boldness to speak Christ's name. The Lord honored this prayer in the same way he honored the laments in the Psalms. Because of this, the believers came to a heightened awareness of God's presence among them, they became emboldened to stand on principle in spite of the resistance they had met, and they experienced a freshly defined unity of purpose (Acts 4:31-37).

Radical New Realities

At the same time, new realities blossom in the New Testament. The most dramatic change revolves around the death and resurrection of Jesus Christ. In the Old Testament, deliverance almost always meant escape from death. By contrast, Jesus came to the earth to die so that through death he could bring eternal life to those who would trust in him. The idea that God's Deliverer would conquer death by dying and then coming back from the dead was inconceivable before Jesus did it. N.T. Wright observes,

> [P]re-Christian Judaism, including the disciples during Jesus's lifetime, never envisaged the death of the Messiah. That is why they never thought of his resurrection, let alone an interim period between such events and the final consummation, still waiting for that sovereign rule to take full effect.[75]

A second unanticipated reality concerns the period we live in now when God invites Jew and non-Jew alike to partake in Christ's grace. Many Old Testament passages speak of God's mercy to the nations, but Hebrew mentality during and after Jesus' ministry struggled with the concept. The Jews expected their Messiah to bring final judgment among the nations and secure Israel's position as the world's dominant political power. In their minds, their covenant relationship would remain theirs exclusively. They were unable to envision an open invitation to the nations to join them to worship a Messiah who had risen from the dead.

The Emergence of Hope on a Global Scale

These first two realities merge into a third, one that involves a far more comprehensive understanding of hope. In the Old Testament, hope was temporal and belonged primarily to those followers who placed their trust in the LORD within the confines of the Jewish covenant.[76] When Jesus ministered on the earth, however, he began to welcome non-Jews into his circle of followers.[77] Because of that, Gentiles who formerly had found themselves shut out found an open invitation to fellowship with Jesus. This ever-growing call continues throughout the New Testament.[78]

Because of Christ's work on the cross and his continuing reign from heaven, combined with his inclusion of Gentiles in the sphere of his salvation, hope has become a shared global phenomenon. As the next chapter will show, hope is more than multi-ethnic. It extends to the cosmos itself.

Therefore, rather than acting as a replacement for the Old Testament, the New Testament becomes a new and unanticipated fulfillment of the promises in the Old.

> That is why, incidentally, the Old Testament must be seen as part of the Christian scripture. I respect those who call the Old Testament the Hebrew Scriptures to acknowledge that they are still the scriptures of a living faith community different from Christianity, but Luke [referring to Jesus' two post-resurrections appearances in the Gospel of Luke 24:13-49] insists that since Jesus really was raised from the dead, the ancient scriptures of Israel must be read

as a story that reaches its climax in Jesus and will then produce its proper fruit not only in Israel but also in Jesus's followers and, through them, in all the world.[79]

The two prerequisites mentioned at the beginning of this book—the necessity for a good God who opposes evil and an all-powerful God who will defeat evil—merge in an entirely unanticipated manner. The ancient story delivered to Israel and witnessed through Jesus' ministry gives us a far more comprehensive understanding of hope.

Jesus, the Good God

Jesus showed himself to be the ultimate manifestation of goodness when he submitted to death on the cross. But his gift was more than a top-down act of pity for the unfortunates. He experienced suffering throughout his lifetime, just like his subjects. He knew their pain on their level. The book of Hebrews states the case this way:

> In the days of his flesh, Jesus offered up prayers and supplications, with loud cries and tears to him who was able to save him from death, and he was heard because of his reverence. Although he was a son, he learned obedience through what he suffered. And being made perfect, he became the source of eternal salvation to all who obey him.

> —Hebrews 5:7-9

Timothy Keller explains this teaching this way:

> God is sovereign over suffering and yet, in teaching unique to the Christian faith among the major religions, God also made himself vulnerable and subject to suffering. The other side of the sovereignty of God is the suffering of God himself...Yes, he is Lord of history, but he is also the vulnerable one who entered that history and became subject to its darkest forces.[80]

Jesus the All-powerful God

By itself, Jesus' willingness to suffer offers only a partial solution to the problem of evil. Submitting to suffering may demonstrate his empathy, but if he wants to conquer evil, he must be stronger than the evil he confronts. He accomplished this by overcoming the greatest expression of evil, death itself.

In overcoming death, Jesus showed himself to be the all-powerful God that he claimed to be. His resurrection and ascension to heaven established his right to claim redemptive rights for the cosmos. Throughout the Old Testament, God had promised to bring justice to the universe. When Jesus rose from the dead, the hope became a paid-in-full guarantee.

These realities provide a platform for God to work in a way that dwarfs the Old Testament writers' expectations. Hope has moved from a political promise for Israel to a cosmic promise for all who believe. God's eternal plan always was global in the largest sense of the word. From the beginning, his plan has extended to the whole cosmos.

Jesus in Waiting

In this time, however, God chooses to withhold his right to judge. Now, he works through circumstances including grief and loss, and calls for us to wait for his final glorification along with him. He is sovereign because he has defeated evil on the cross. But he is also empathetic in the deepest possible sense. Therefore, as he waits to judge the world, he invites us to wait with him. This calling allows us to embrace the two realities of faith.

- Because of the promise implicit in Jesus' fulfilled mission, we have cause to hope, even when suffering and pain threaten to break us. We look forward to a brighter future.
- At the same time, grief and loss remain realities. In this life, we continue to mourn.

The purpose of Jesus' work of grace was not to eliminate injustice and suffering…yet. For the present, he reaches out to us with a message of grace. The author of Hebrews writes,

159

> At present, we do not yet see everything in subjection to him. But we see him who for a little while was made lower than the angels, namely Jesus, crowned with glory and honor because of the suffering of death, so that by the grace of God he might taste death for everyone.
>
> —Hebrews 2:8-9

The fact that Jesus has tasted death for everyone means that his apparent hesitance to eliminate suffering from the world is neither arbitrary nor sadistic. He knows what pain means, and he gives certain comfort when we suffer. Conversely, suffering becomes a vehicle through which we can begin to understand what Jesus endured. Andrew Schmutzer observes, "Even extreme suffering now—now—opens us to the depth of God's relational commitment [to us]."[81] When we experience the same kind of deep pain that Jesus experienced, we gain a deeper stake in his presence with us because we become more aware of his ability to sympathize with us. Suffering drives us toward a level of fellowship with him that is impossible by any other means.

Therefore, future eternal hope becomes more concrete in the New Testament than the Old Testament because the New Testament understands Jesus' death, resurrection, and ascension in both their historical and eternal meanings. Historically, we bear witness to Jesus' call, "Follow me," even in suffering. Jesus never promises a pain-free life.

From the eternal perspective, we look to a future in which all suffering will disappear in Jesus' fulfilled grace. According to Wright,

> When God saves people in this life, by working through his Spirit to bring them to faith and by leading them to follow Jesus in discipleship, prayer, holiness, hope, and love, such people are designed—it isn't too strong a word—to be a sign and foretaste of what God wants to do for the entire cosmos.[82]

This truth has two implications. The first points to what we know already. As long as we are on this side of eternity, we will continue to experience suffering. Our praise will continue to carry the memory of lament. In this life, we wait for his promised return, when he takes away our tears once for all.

The second implication gives us a reason for hope in suffering. Jesus gives meaning to our suffering. When we suffer, we bear witness to his suffering in the world. When we show confidence during times of difficulty, we give the world reason to consider Jesus as the Lord he is. Hope becomes our foundation for joy. For that reason, the remainder of this book will focus on our eternal hope.

Journal Entry

In the issue that causes me the most personal pain, how can I speak to myself in a way that gives me a perspective of the bigger picture? _____

_____

_____

_____

CHAPTER 13

Romans 8:18-29
The Theology of Hope

The riddle and insight of biblical faith is the awareness
that only anguish leads to life, only grieving leads to joy,
and only embraced endings permit new beginnings.[83]

Why do faithful people suffer?

The question rings with the same melancholy in the New Testament as it does in the Old. It sounds throughout the Scripture in one way or another. We have examined some of the questions regarding suffering in the books of Job and the Psalms, but this book represents only a sampling on the subject. Almost every book in the Old Testament grapples with these issues. All three sections of the Hebrew Bible, the *Torah* (or Teaching), the Prophets (which include what we call the Historical Books), and the Wisdom Books, address the question.

We have examined some of the Wisdom Literature on the subject. Questions regarding righteousness and justice abound in the Wisdom Literature. Similarly, the historical literature "seeks to 'render an account' of the past—to provide an explanation...for the circumstances or conditions of the historian's day"[84] in a manner consistent with theological expectations. Furthermore, "Torah is virtually synonymous with divine Wisdom...and in this sense bears on the character and structure of the whole created order."[85]

When we enter the New Testament, we encounter the issues again. The first four books of the New Testament, known as the Gospels, all tell about Jesus' life, death, and resurrection in narrative form.[86] One of the most important issues in the Gospels revolves around the question regarding Jesus' suffering. Jesus' followers believed he would restore justice and bring in the everlasting kingdom God had promised. They looked only for a mighty God who would eliminate his enemies.

Jesus had a different idea. During his ministry on the earth, he told his disciples repeatedly that ultimate glory would have to wait because final deliverance is to take place much later in history. His mission was to suffer, die, and come back to life to redeem a people to call his own, from both Jews and Gentiles. By sacrificing his life to conquer death, he set an entirely new dynamic into motion.

History and Hope in Romans 8:18-25

The Apostle Paul's writings answer the global issues in the *Torah,* the Prophets, the Wisdom books, and the Gospels from the perspective of Jesus' resurrection from the dead. The eighth chapter of Romans acknowledges human suffering while it offers one of the great hymns of praise regarding God's ultimate plan to redeem his creation and deliver his people from suffering.

In this chapter, a fundamental contribution to understanding suffering from a New Testament perspective involves two realities. One is history, and the other is hope. For this discussion, we can say that history encompasses our experiences, with all their pain and grief. It includes everything that happens to us, whether good or evil.

In this life, we are bound by history's reality. We do not need to go beyond our experience to know that good and pleasurable things are temporary. Movies run their course and begin to roll the credits. Books reach the last page. Vacations end. Family members die. Friendships fade with time or distance. Nothing that is pleasurable in this life lasts forever, for the simple reason that God has made "forever" something of a different essence from history. Eternity in the New Testament sense is not an extension of history, *ad infinitum.* It is an entirely new state of being that will call for the transformation of the cosmos and those who live in it.

The second reality enters here. Our expectation for this transformation of history involves hope. We know from the Bible that Jesus will return to set history right because his resurrection has taken place in history. This truth gives us hope. In short, hope is the settled conviction that God will lead us to a glorious end. Hope makes three conclusions about the meaning of history:

- First, a big story exists. History has a meaning.
- Second, the story has a happy ending.
- Third, we will be there when the story ends.

When we possess hope, joy can thrive in the midst of pain. N.T. Wright expresses the truth this way:

> Hope is what you get when you suddenly realize that a different worldview is possible, a worldview in which the rich, the powerful, and the unscrupulous do not after all have the last word.[87]

New Testament worship recognizes both history and hope. As long as history continues, we will have reason to mourn. On the other hand, we have the promise that deliverance will come in eternity. The promise reignites a purpose for living because where hope reigns, joy becomes possible once again. And where joy is present, praise is certain to follow.

Romans 8:18-25 is a short passage that covers the span of time from the beginning of history to Christ's return when he brings our anticipated hope to a conclusion. It addresses the issues in the *Torah,* the Prophets, the Wisdom books, and the Gospels. The passage is an expression of worship in the fullest sense. Because it begins in history and ends in hope, it finds reason to praise in the midst of pain. This concept is important enough to quote the entire section. I have labeled the two parts for clarity.

Part 1: History:

> For I consider that the sufferings of this present time are not worth comparing with the glory that is to be revealed to us. For the creation waits with eager longing for the revealing of the sons of God. For the creation was subjected to futility, not willingly, but because of him who subjected it, in hope that the creation itself will be set free from its bondage to decay and obtain the freedom of the glory of the children of God. For we know that the whole creation has been groaning together in the pains of childbirth until now.
>
> —Romans 8:18-22

Part 2: Hope:

And not only the creation but we ourselves, who have the firstfruits of the Spirit, groan inwardly as we wait eagerly for adoption as sons, the redemption of our bodies. For in this hope we were saved. Now hope that is seen is not hope. For who hopes for what he sees? But if we hope for what we do not see, we wait for it with patience.

—Romans 8:23-25

History in Perspective, (Romans 8:18-21)

Paul has not slipped into romantic idealism. Throughout the passage, he has one foot planted in the present time and the other resting in the future. In the first section, he writes, "For the creation waits with eager longing for the revealing of the sons of God....For we know that the whole creation has been groaning together in the pains of childbirth until now."

Against the reality of present-day suffering, he gives us balancing perspective. Christ owns eternity. Our lives may be measured, but eternity never ends. Therefore, even severe suffering is finite, but our glory will last forever. When we compare the two realities in this way, suffering begins to fall into perspective. The pain we experience now, Paul says, is unworthy to be compared with our future.

Everything in this section stands on these two truths. In verses 19-21 Paul follows history back to the creation. He says the creation was "subject to futility" (Romans 8:20) and put under "bondage to corruption" (Romans 8:21). Certain questions arise when we read this passage:

- What do the terms, "subject to futility" and "bondage to corruption," mean?
- When did this futility and corruption occur?
- What made it happen?

All these questions reach back to the beginning of history. In the first chapter of Genesis, the Bible records the seven days of creation. Day after day, as God observes what he has made, he sees, "It was good." At the end of the section, Genesis records, "And God saw everything that he had made, and behold, it was very good" (Genesis 1:31).

But that which was good was to be short lived. As this book discussed in Chapter 3, God gave the man and woman he had created a simple test to see whether they would obey or rebel. The test involved a single act. They could choose to trust God's word about the fruit they were forbidden to eat, or they could disregard the warning and eat it.

They chose the latter and severed the innocent relationship they had with their God. From that point on, all of history fell under the shadow of the first man and woman's rebellion. Here is the place where the creation became "subject to futility" under its "bondage to corruption." We cannot stress the consequences of this too strongly. The man and woman's rebellion was the shot heard round the cosmos. Theologically, we call this the Fall, which means the tragic disruption that occurred because of history's first rebellion. Here is what happened according to the Genesis account.

- **The Original Design for the Cosmos:** The LORD God created the man and woman as marriage partners and placed them in the middle of a paradise. He gave them the responsibility to tend the garden and also gave them permission to eat any fruit they wanted except for the one forbidden fruit (Genesis 2:15-24).
- **Human responsibility in the cosmos:** The only prohibited fruit was the "tree of the knowledge of good and evil" in the middle of the garden." In the Lord's words, "in the day that you eat of it, you will surely die" (Genesis 2:17).
- **The Origin of Rebellion:** The serpent, "more crafty than any other beast of the field that the LORD God had made" (Genesis 3:1), spoke to the woman and twisted the truth about the tree. The lie was that she would escape death. In the serpent's words, "God knows that when you eat of it your eyes will be opened, and you will be like God, knowing good and evil" (Genesis 3:5).
- **The Consequences of Rebellion:** The woman then took the fruit and shared it with her husband. When this happened, "their eyes were opened" (Genesis 3:7), but only to the degree that they realized they were naked. Nakedness in the Bible always implies vulnerability. When trust is involved, as the case it was in their original state, nakedness was benign. The man and woman's rebellion transformed their innocence to shame because of their

breach of trust. They made loincloths for themselves and hid from God's presence (Genesis 3:8-9) until the LORD called them out.

To this point, Genesis is silent about the creation being "subject to futility." That takes place in the next few verses. When God confronts the serpent, the man, and the woman, he pronounces judgment on each. Two of the judgments involve curses. In the first, God cursed the serpent directly.

> "Because you have done this,
>> cursed are you above all livestock
>> and above all beasts of the field;
> on your belly you shall go,
>> and dust you shall eat all the days of your life."

—Genesis 3:14

When the LORD spoke to Adam, the curse defaulted to the ground. Adam had been the chief caretaker of the Garden. Tending the Garden had been a means to fulfillment as a man. Adam's vocation would turn against him.

> "Because you have listened to the voice of your wife
>> and have eaten of the tree
>> of which I commanded you,
>> 'You shall not eat of it,'
> cursed is the ground because of you;
>> in pain you shall eat of it all the days of your life....
>
> By the sweat of your face
>> you shall eat bread,
> till you return to the ground,
>> for out of it you were taken;
> for you are dust,
>> and to dust you shall return."

—Genesis 3:17, 19

When Paul talks about the creation being subject to futility, he refers to God's placing it under a curse. "For the creation was subjected to futility,

167

not willingly, *but because of him who subjected it, in hope that the creation itself will be set free from its bondage to decay and obtain the freedom of the glory of the children of God* (Romans 8:20-21, emphasis added). This statement makes three important distinctions.

- The creation's subjection to futility occurred because of God's actions on it.
- "Futility" involved a much deeper bondage to decay, signified by the man returning to the dust from which he was created (Genesis 3:19).
- Hope arises out of the tragedy. Along with the subjection came the hope that the creation ultimately will be set free from its bondage to decay and will "obtain the freedom of the glory of the children of God."

In Genesis, the promise to which Paul refers appears as a glimmer of hope in the midst of judgment. The account continues this thread. "And the LORD God made for Adam and for his wife garments of skins and clothed them" (Genesis 3:21). Their coverings required sacrificial animals. The innocent had to die on behalf of the guilty. They also demonstrated God's determination to reestablish a loving relationship with the people who had spurned him. We inhabit a wounded world, with death all around us, but a day is coming when God will set the creation free from the curse.

Hope in Perspective, (Romans 8:22-25)

Hope is not the cessation of suffering. It is the promise of deliverance in the midst of pain. Paul expresses hope in full view of the universal suffering. He never jumps out of history to tout hope.

> For we know that the whole creation has been groaning together in the pains of childbirth until now. And not only the creation, but we ourselves, who have the firstfruits of the Spirit, groan inwardly as we wait eagerly for adoption as sons, the redemption of our bodies.
>
> —Romans 8:22-23

Hope is more than wishful thinking. One Bible expositor described it as the joy we experience when we consciously understand that God will bring us through the difficulty. He is right. More importantly, hope rises out of hopelessness. In Genesis, for example, during the brief time that the world existed without sin, it also lived without hope. In a sin-free world, no one needed to hope for anything better. Only when a crisis came, did hope come to mean something significant. The day that God covered his children's nakedness with animal skins, the innocent dying for the guilty, hope began.

Hope as a cause for joy reached its pinnacle after Jesus' resurrection from the dead. His resurrection became the vehicle by which the Father has given us what Paul calls "the firstfruits of the Spirit" (Romans 8:23). This term means the presence of the Holy Spirit in the believer's life. It is the last and most sure guarantee that God will fulfill his promise to redeem us once for all. Just as the early crop marked the certainty of the rest of the harvest, the presence of the Holy Spirit marks the guarantee of our ultimate deliverance from corruption.

Romans 8:24, the concluding statement for the section, shows the intersection point for history and hope. "For in this hope we have been saved. Now hope that is seen is not hope. For who hopes for what he sees?" Hope recognizes the necessity for history while it anticipates a glorious future. It makes the prospect of our ultimate resurrection both desirable and necessary. The hope of the resurrection gains its beauty in the presence of suffering. If we only flit from one victory to the next, why bother to hope for what God promised in our future? "Life is good, Lord. You can hold off on the resurrection for a while." Substantive hope lives through the pain. N.T. Wright says this:

> The Bible as a whole thus does what it does best when it is read from the perspective of the new creation....It is the book whose whole narrative is about the new creation, that is, about resurrection, so that when each of the gospels ends with the raising of Jesus from the dead, and when Revelation ends with new heavens and new earth populated by God's people risen from the dead, this should come not as a surprise but as the ultimate fulfillment of what the story had been about all along.[88]

Along with the rest of the Bible, Paul says we groan while we wait eagerly for the redemption of our bodies. We recognize that something better waits for us. To put it another way, if we live in the middle of "Party hearty," we live only in the moment. How often, for example, do we ponder theology during the New Year's Eve countdown? Theological issues matter most when history rages against us.

Hope becomes our discipline during pain. "Now hope that is seen is not hope. For who hopes for what he sees? But if we hope for what we do not see, we wait for it with patience" (Romans 8:24-25). By definition, hope requires us to focus on that which will come.

The Necessity to Embrace Hope in our Return to Praise

History and hope balance each other, and both are necessary for meaningful praise. Hope gains substance only when we acknowledge the reality of history, and history has true meaning only when we view it in light of the hope to come.

For the Christian, history is never all there is, because God has promised a greater future. We look forward in hope to the fulfillment of his promise. On the other hand, hope requires us to maintain a meaningful lock on history. If we abandon either perspective, we eliminate our ability to live meaningfully as Christians.

History without Hope

Suppose, for example, that we lose sight of hope and try to live only in history. The inevitable result will be that pleasure will become isolated from any larger context and degenerate into desirable stimulus. As one author notes, "Pleasurable satisfaction is heavily dependent on external circumstances (for example, performing well in a game or even at church, or enjoying a movie). As such it is relatively unstable and comes and goes with the flux of a person's circumstances."[89]

The biblical writers understood this. The book of Ecclesiastes in the Old Testament is a journal of one man's attempt to find ultimate meaning exclusively in history, absent any higher guiding authority. The author writes,

I said in my heart, "I have acquired great wisdom, surpassing all who were over Jerusalem before me, and my heart has had great experience of wisdom and knowledge." And I applied my heart to know wisdom and to know madness and folly. I perceived that this also is but a striving after wind.

For in much wisdom is much vexation,
> and he who increases knowledge increases sorrow.

I said in my heart, "Come now, I will test you with pleasure; enjoy yourself." But behold, this also was vanity. I said of laughter, "it is mad," and of pleasure, "What use is it?"

—Ecclesiastes 1:16-2:2

History saturates Ecclesiastes. The writer's efforts to find meaning "under the sun," or from history alone, always end in futility. A life lived in history alone is devoid of hope.

The reality is as true in our time as it was when the Bible was coming into being. Modern atheism, for example, defines reality as material cause and effect in the absence of any outside direction. By definition, hope cannot exist in such a world. In 1978 and 1979, astrophysicist Carl Sagan produced *Cosmos*, a thirteen-part PBS series on the natural history of the universe. At the beginning of every episode, his voice-over mantra told his audience, "The cosmos is all that is, or ever was, or ever will be." The declaration was Dr. Sagan's line in the sand. Friends were welcome to stay and enjoy the show. Those who believed in anything other than the uniformity of causes in a closed system were free to change the channel.

With the help of the series' ethereal music, Sagan turned atheism into a utopian ideal. In a doxology that praised matter plus time plus chance, he lulled viewers into starry-eyed wonder as they pondered the "billions and billions of years" required for humanity to come into being. Sagan's evolutionary optimism counterfeited biblical hope. Just give the cosmos enough time and enough matter, and anything can happen. He was the evolutionist's romantic.

Now, going on forty years later, the allure has turned to dust. The polemic that comes out of the mouths of the present generation of radical atheists like Douglas Adams, Christopher Hitchens, or Richard Dawkins has replaced the romance with a far bleaker picture. Dawkins writes,

> On the contrary, if the universe were just electrons and selfish genes, [then] meaningless tragedies...are exactly what we should expect, along with equally meaningless good fortune. Such a universe would be neither evil nor good in intention. It would manifest no intentions of any kind. In a universe of blind physical forces and genetic replication, some people are going to get hurt, other people are going to get lucky, and you won't find any rhyme or reason in it, nor any justice. [90]

When we deny the legitimacy of hope, wonder becomes the next fatality. Forget awe. Dawkins' "selfish...meaningless tragedies" and "equally meaningless good fortune" become the mainstay of our existence. Interestingly, Dawkins and others like him, the ones who manage to "get lucky," tend to flaunt their fortune in a way that begins to become disingenuous after a while. Meanwhile, those who suffer tragedy reside in a kind of modern-day karma. How ironic that the "lucky" ones not only are the first to deny "any rhyme or reason...nor any justice," but also are the first to become incensed at those who look for rhyme, reason, and justice under God. In the atheists' universe, the search for meaning is a moral crime.

Hope without History

The other extreme, which often occurs in the Christian camp, is hope outside of historical context. Without a connection to history, optimism degenerates to mindlessness. By "mindless," I do not mean unthinking, but the kind of hope that allows only praise, without tolerance for lament. Mindless hope denies us the right to question God at all because it assumes that doubts point to a deficiency in our faith. Hope-only thinking is just a nice way of saying, "All praise all the time." It denies us the privilege of calling out to God for a miracle. Mindless hope detests grief and lament. But when we stop crying, "How long, O Lord?" we close the doors for the

Lord to enter history. A recent blog by Sam Williamson expresses the issue in concrete terms.

> I once met with a man—let's call him Nathan—who described himself as a "recovering charismatic." He was open to it; but his experience of modern worship gave him pause.
>
> As he grew up, his mother frenetically flitted from one worship experience to the next.
>
> After Toronto she visited Florida, then Bethel Church, and then anywhere she heard "something" was happening.
>
> Worship music unceasingly blared throughout the house. She seemed to need its euphoric "oomph" to motivate her for the tiniest of tasks. Wiping kitchen counters took the combined efforts of Matt Redman, Chris Tomlin, and Paul Baloche....But she remained anxious, fearful, self-concerned, and neglectful of her husband and sons. She'd say, "I just want to go where God is working," but it really seemed she just wanted an escape, a place where her problems could be sedated.
>
> After describing all this, Nathan added, *"A friend of mine became a crack addict. Frankly I didn't see much difference between him and my mom. They got their highs in different ways, and their lives remained a mess."*
>
> *"I wonder,"* he continued, *"if modern worship is like a cocaine rush."*[91]

Praise without lament is nothing more than hope divorced from history, which amounts to a denial that the present reality is evil. It is purposeful, selective amnesia because it denies grief and lament, the very features that root our feet in fact.

Hope in the biblical sense is far more than a mere vision for a better future. It recognizes God's rule over both the present and the future. Hope acknowledges that God plans to fulfill his promise to change the future, and it acknowledges that he still controls our current circumstances. In other words, hope looks to a better tomorrow without ignoring the suffering in the present.

Ultimately, the reality of hope becomes a subversive act against those who try to control by numbing. By definition, the character of hope calls us to recognize the evil in the present and to call for its demise. As soon as we hope for something "better" than the evil around us, we expose the current evil for what it is. Brueggemann observes,

> [T]he real criticism [of the present reality] begins in the capacity to grieve because that is the most visceral announcement that things are not right. Only in the empire [i.e. the powers that rule in history while they deny the existence of hope] are we pressed and urged and invited to pretend that things are all right—either in the dean's office or in our marriage or in the hospital room. And as long as the empire can keep the pretense alive that things are all right, there will be no real grieving and no serious criticism.[92]

Conclusion

The following are some observations on hope. They are not meant to be exhaustive.

1. Hope is not intended only to pacify us while we wait for eternity. Issues related to justice require us to protest. They are as connected to history in the New Testament as they were in the Psalms. In the Old Testament, Moses delivered the Israelites from Egyptian bondage in Exodus by exposing its evil. In modern history, William Wilberforce devoted his life to abolishing slavery in England, both because he understood its cruelty and because he held the hope that his efforts would be ultimately successful. Many carry on similar work in the pro-life movement today. Every Christian humanitarian effort in history has dared to pit a hopeful dream against a brutal reality.

2. Hope recognizes that God plans useful purpose for our pain. The recognition may be as simple as the realization that yearning may have to carry us through our circumstances. Comfort may or may not remain with us. Eternity shines most brightly when we recognize its source in God's promises (Romans 8:25).

3. Discontentment in history is necessary for the vision and growth of future hope. If all the answers to our questions were to become apparent to us today, we would lack any reason to long for something better.
4. Sometimes hope remains a distant prospect. God reveals a plan for redemption, but he does not always give us the details. The book of Job shows that we must wait for the answers to the cosmic *why* questions. Hope grows where answers remain elusive.

Journal Entry

What do you mourn? _____

_____

_____

_____

How does the presence of hope affect the way you mourn? _____

_____

_____

_____

If you mourn something that is unjust or needs to be changed, how do you plan to work to change it? _____

_____

_____

_____

CHAPTER 14

Knowing the God of Hope

"Then he isn't safe?" said Lucy.
"Safe?" said Mister Beaver....Who said anything about safe?
'Course he isn't safe. But he's good. He's the King, I tell you."[93]

I have written this book for anyone who is open to the idea that a God exists who is loving enough to care for his creatures and sufficiently powerful to make restitution for the evil in the world. If you have read this far, I would like to invite you to enter into a personal relationship with the God of hope.

Who is God?

The biblical book of Acts is a history of the early church, including the missionary work of the Apostle Paul from AD 34-68. In Acts 17, Paul is in Athens, one of the cultural and economic centers of the ancient world. As he walks about the area, seeing temples and altars throughout the city dedicated to the various gods, a particular one catches his eye. It bears the inscription, "To the Unknown God" (Acts 17:23). Obviously, the people in the city are conscientious and careful to avoid offending this deity. Paul's sermon proclaims him as the God of the Bible and explains why everyone needs to know who he is. Here is a summary of what Paul says about the God of the Bible in this sermon delivered in classic Greek oratorical fashion. [94] He begins his declaration of the God of creation in terms amenable to natural theology.

> "The God who made the world and everything in it, being
> Lord of heaven and earth, does not live in temples made
> by man, nor is he served by human hands, as though he

needed anything, since he himself gives to all mankind life and breath and everything.

—Acts 17:25

The God of the Bible is our Creator, the one who created order in the cosmos and the biosphere. Unlike the ancient gods of the pantheon, the Creator does not need our admiration to feed his sense of esteem. He is self-sufficient as God. At the same time, he seeks to build a relationship with his creatures. Paul goes on to say,

"And he made from one man every nation of mankind to live on all the face of the earth, having determined allotted periods and the boundaries of their dwelling place, that they should seek God, in the hope that they might feel their way toward him and find him.

—Acts 17:26-27a

In proclaiming common descent of the nations from a single human ancestor, Paul acknowledges unity and diversity among the peoples. Humanity has diversified into different cultures and languages, but they share a common origin. Because of this, God is universally knowable. People who seek him can find him. Paul supports this assertion by appealing to insights from two Greek poets.

"Yet he is actually not far from each one of us, for 'In him we live and move and have our being';[95] as even some of your own poets have said, 'For we are indeed his offspring.'[96]

—Acts 17:27b-28

This book's premise affirms Paul's statement. God is near. When crisis strikes, our overwhelming natural inclination is to seek God to find comfort, because we know that he can help. When our world falls apart, we run to God. Paul concludes his case from natural theology with these words:

> "Being then God's offspring, we ought not to think that the divine being is like gold or silver or stone, an image formed by the art and imagination of man.
>
> —Acts 17:29

Athens was given over to theistic practice. Temples and monuments to the gods dotted the landscape. Paul draws the Athenian philosophers to consider a greater God, one who is beyond the need to be coddled by human-made spectacles in gold and silver.

The Bible and the Question of Judgment

Paul's strategy is to move from natural theology to biblical declaration. He does this when he declares Jesus' resurrection. This final point makes a case for the biblical Christ.

> "The times of ignorance God overlooked, but now he commands all people everywhere to repent, because he has fixed a day on which he will judge the world in righteousness by a man whom he has appointed; and of this he has given assurance to all by raising him from the dead."
>
> —Acts 17:30-31

What Paul calls the times of ignorance comprise world history before Jesus' ministry on the earth. Now, however, since the Bible has recorded his life, death, and resurrection, the message goes out to the world that he will return to judge the world. We must acknowledge him as the supreme authority in the universe.

This message flew in the face of Paul's audience. The people to whom he spoke were Stoics and Epicureans (Acts 17:18). While each group displayed an intense interest in the problem of evil, they also held an equally passionate antagonism to the biblical solution for evil. The Epicureans were materialistic philosophers who denied any divine presence in the world. Any fear of judgment was anathema to them, so they sought diversion as a means to avoid their fear. Epicurus encouraged the study of nature to bolster the diversion from fear. In a real way, the Epicureans became the first naturalists. In a materialistic world, the Epicureans insisted, death is final. By definition, resurrection does not take place. [97]

The Stoics believed in an immaterial power, in the form of an impersonal Logos. Evil was less a flaw to be remedied than an integral part of the universe. Suffering arises when we try to hold too tightly to material objects. Life's primary goal, therefore, is to avoid too tight a grip on material possessions or relationships. When we die, our body and soul continue to exist in different forms.[98] For them, a belief in a bodily resurrection is meaningless.

Jesus' resurrection is unappealing among many thinking people. The moment Paul mentions it to the Athenian philosophers, his audience boos him down, leaving him unable to finish his sermon. Nonetheless, he refuses to flinch, for the simple reason that the doctrine of the resurrection and return of Jesus is the capstone in the biblical teaching regarding God's solution for the problem of evil. Commenting on the importance of the resurrection, John Blanchard writes,

> As far as the future history of the world is concerned, nothing is stated more often or more emphatically than the Second Coming of Christ. It is mentioned no fewer than 300 times in the New Testament alone, which works out at once in every thirteen verses from Matthew to Revelation.[99]

Neither Epicureanism nor Stoicism could accept the biblical resurrection. Consequently, neither view had an answer to the problem of evil. The message in the Bible is clear. God's intention to "judge the world in righteousness" means bringing final justice to the world. Job and his friends argued about its design. David longed for justice in Psalm 109/110. The psalmists cried out against the injustices they experienced. In his death and resurrection, Jesus provided satisfaction for their deepest longings.

For this reason, Jesus Christ has become the focal point of world history. He demonstrated perfect empathy for those who suffer because he suffered himself. He also paid the debt for the sinful acts of the wicked. Paul writes, "For there is one God, and there is one mediator between God and men, the man Christ Jesus, who gave himself as a ransom for all, which is the testimony given at the proper time" (1 Timothy 2:5-6).

In dying and rising from the dead, Jesus completed the work required to solve the problem of evil. He is the Champion who overthrows the wicked. Biblical commentator Peter T. O'Brien writes, "Christ is the one *in whom* God chooses to sum up the cosmos, the one in whom he restores harmony to the universe. He is the focal point, not simply the means, the instrument, or the functionary through whom all this occurs."[100]

Jesus at Every Point in History

This book has outlined a brief global history of hope from a biblical perspective. Biblical history has included some pivotal events. These have been as follows:

- God's original creation of a perfect heaven and earth
- The entrance of moral evil and corruption into the cosmos
- The suffering that resulted from the entrance of moral evil into the world
- The promise that justice through Jesus would include redemption as well as punishment
- The hope for the ultimate triumph of good at the conclusion of history

According to the Bible, Jesus has been active at every one of these points. This section will review the points and show Jesus' presence in them.

God's original creation of a perfect heaven and earth: The Bible opens with the words, "In the beginning, God created the heavens and the earth" (Genesis 1:1). In the original language, the word for *created* is *bara'*. It means *to create* in the absolute sense, meaning to call something into being. The word is used only of God. No one else creates.

Of course, this statement runs in the face of our modern scientific notions. Evolution, the dominant modern Western definition of reality, denies the existence of God.[101] If we consider the logical alternatives, however, the notion of an eternal Creator is far less frivolous than what the evolutionists claim. When we discuss the issue of ultimate origins, we must acknowledge two logical possibilities. Either something has had to exist forever, or something has to have come from nothing.

Modern science, which cannot tolerate an eternal Creator, has opted for the second option, the assumption that the universe spontaneously appeared (out of nothing, by the way) during the cosmic event known as the Big Bang. Without guidance or rules, the cosmos fashioned itself into an orderly entity that has generated life and intelligence. Science, then, in trying to oppose biblical creation, affirms the same sudden appearance of the material universe.

When we compare the most fundamental tenets of evolution with creation, we find that each attempts to answer the same basic questions. Each view offers an explanation for the universe's existence, and each seeks to explain the order in the cosmos. And—Dawkins notwithstanding—each offers doxology to its chosen creative force. In other words, each is equally religious at its core.

Of course, we would expect a religious affirmation like this from those who believe in the Bible. Praise to God for his creative acts appears throughout the Bible. But scientific works can be equally doxological. The following is an extended quote from Paul R. Lawrence and Nitin Nohria in their book, *Driven: How Human Nature Shapes Our Choices*. The quote shows the authors' devotion to evolution's dogma and its claim to wonder.

> In 1970 one of the authors went on safari in Kenya and Tanzania. Four scenes from that trip are indelibly etched in memory. The first was a long talk with Jane Goodall at her campsite. As a pioneer of the study of chimpanzees in their natural habitat, she laid the foundation for modern knowledge of the behavior of chimpanzees, the closest living relative of the species that split from the primate line to start the multimillion-year evolution to modern humans.
>
> The second was a stop at Olduvai Gorge, where Mary Leaky pointed out the spot where she and her husband George Leaky had discovered the 1.75 million-year-old skull of Zinjanthropus man. These remains, along with subsequent hominid [the family *Hominidae,* which includes humans and their ancestral primates] finds, have helped scholars reconstruct the evolutionary steps leading to modern *Homo sapiens.*

The third was an opportunity to visit a Masai village to get a brief feel for the strength and sophistication of their hunter-gatherer-herder way of life. Tribes such as this offer the best available approximation of the way of life of the biologically modern humans who, as hunter-gatherers, moved out of Africa approximately seventy thousand years ago fully equipped to thrive in all parts of the globe.

The final scene was a dawn's-light view of huge clusters of herbivores—wildebeests, zebras, gazelles, giraffes, and many others—moving gracefully in a vast grassland. In their midst were two Masai warriors, spears over their shoulders, striding with total confidence across the huge plain. The scene epitomized the environment where modern human genes were formed and selected. It felt like Eden.[102]

One would think that a declaration of belief so opposed to the biblical perspective would find a less ironic metaphor than Eden. In the end, however, the picture reflects our need for praise. Doxology is the same whether it lies in the Psalms or Carl Sagan's repeated lauding of "billions and billions of years" on his 1980 PBS *Cosmos* series.

The entrance of moral evil and corruption into the cosmos and the suffering that resulted from it: Unfortunately, the evolutionist's Eden fails to offer a real solution for the problem of evil in the world. We saw earlier that the problem of evil is real to both theists and non-theists. Part of the reason Charles Darwin is such an important figure in the history of evolution thought is that he tried to address both issues, the scientific question about the process of life, and the moral issue about the meaning of life. Cornelius G. Hunter comments,

> Darwin's theory of evolution was very much a solution to the problem of natural evil—a theodicy [a theological justification of God's goodness in the presence of evil]. The problem had confounded thinkers for centuries. They needed to distance God to clear him of any evil doings. Darwin solved the problem by coming up with a natural law that he argued could account for evil. Natural selection, operating blindly on a pool of biological

diversity, according to Darwin, could produce nature's carnage and waste.[103]

The solution looks brilliant at first. If natural evil is part of the mechanism of the universe, a position lauded by Darwinists, then the problem of moral evil is eliminated by default. Even moral actions are explainable by natural causes. Such a solution looks good on paper, but it cannot stand by itself. "Evil," though present and recognizable, becomes indefinable in moral terms. It exists only as part of the structure of the world.

At its logical endpoint, empathy disappears. While we may succeed in ridding ourselves of those nagging "why" questions, we also leave ourselves lacking values. In a universe consisting of blind physical forces, nothing *matters*.

The biblical account, on the other hand, recognizes natural and moral evil[104] and offers flesh-and-blood responses to it. The Bible offers both purpose and the promise of redemption. It offers hope through Jesus because Jesus is the one who takes on the theodicy question from the beginning. For example, the Apostle John, borrowing from the book of Genesis, writes,

> In the beginning was the Word [God's Son, who would become Jesus in the Incarnation], and the Word was with God, and the Word was God. He was in the beginning with God. All things were made through him, and without him was not any thing made that was made.
>
> —John 1:1-3

Paul makes the same claim about Jesus the Son. He is the Creator, and he creates with a purpose.

> He [the Son] is the image of the invisible God, the firstborn of all creation. For by him all things were created, in heaven and on earth, visible and invisible, whether thrones or dominions or rulers or authorities—all things were created through him and for him.
>
> —Colossians 1:15-16

Jesus created all things in order to reveal himself to the world as the one being that is capable of solving the problem of evil. The Apostle Peter wrote this to the first century believers who faced persecution for their beliefs. "Conduct yourselves with fear throughout the time of your exile, knowing that you were ransomed from the futile ways inherited from your forefathers, not with perishable things such as silver or gold, but with the precious blood of Christ, like that of a lamb without blemish or spot. He was foreknown [meaning foreordained] before the foundation of the world *but was made manifest in the last times for the sake of you*" (1 Peter 1:18-20, emphasis added).

The promise that justice through Jesus would include redemption as well as punishment: The book of Job shows that God alone is capable of dispensing justice in the world. The Book of Psalms shows that he cares enough to bring justice. When we follow the Bible forward to Jesus' ministry on the earth, we find a new and unanticipated truth. Jesus became the focal point for both justice and mercy. He died on behalf of the rebellious so that he might give them the gift of eternal grace. In doing so, he became the champion of justice. Paul writes in Philippians,

> Have this mind among yourselves, which is yours in Christ Jesus, who, though he was in the form of God, did not count equality with God a thing to be grasped, but emptied himself, by taking the form of a servant, being born in the likeness of men. And being found in human form, he humbled himself by becoming obedient to the point of death, even death on a cross. Therefore God has highly exalted him and bestowed on him the name that is above every name, so that at the name of Jesus every knee should bow, in heaven and on earth and under the earth, and every tongue confess that Jesus Christ is Lord, to the glory of God the Father.
>
> —Philippians 2:5-11

The promise for the ultimate triumph of good at the conclusion of history: The promise that Jesus will restore the cosmos is more than just a future vision. It encompasses all of biblical history, beginning with the Garden of Eden, where God chose to fellowship with the man and the woman. That fellowship was simultaneously the most precious and the most fragile thing that Adam and his wife could have. Commenting on the Garden of Eden, J.H. Walton writes,

> When we see that creation as a whole was understood in terms of a cosmic temple complex, it would be logical to understand the garden as the antechamber to the holy of holies....With this understanding, it can be appreciated that in the aftermath of the Fall, the greatest loss was not access to paradise; it was to God's presence.[105]

When Adam and his wife disobeyed, they lost both paradise and God's fellowship. Jumping forward in history, Jesus' personal sacrifice on the cross laid the groundwork to restore both his people and his creation. The last two chapters of the Bible show both aspects of the restoration when Jesus eliminates all evil from the world at the end of time and ushers in a new paradise, unimaginably greater than the first. Here is part of what he writes about the eternal presence of Jesus descending from heaven to the earth in the New Jerusalem.

> Then came one of the seven angels who had the seven bowls full of the seven last plagues and spoke to me, saying, "Come, I will show you the Bride, the wife of the Lamb." And he carried me away in the Spirit to a great, high mountain, and showed me the holy city Jerusalem coming down out of heaven from God, having the glory of God, its radiance like a most rare jewel, like a jasper, clear as crystal.... And I saw no temple in the city, for its temple is the Lord God the Almighty and the Lamb. And the city has no need of sun or moon to shine on it, for the glory of God gives it light, and its lamp is the Lamb. By its light will the nations walk, and the kings of the earth will bring their glory into it, and its gates will never be shut by day—and there will be no night there.

> —Revelation 21:9-11, 22-25

As Christians, we take this hope seriously. If the world is to have

185

ultimate meaning—that is, if the problem of evil is to be resolved once for all—then these things must take place. Speaking about God's cosmic creative and moral task, O'Brien writes, "Before the foundation of the world [God the Father] chose a people for himself in Christ and predestined them to be his children (Eph. 1:4-5)....And he who *created* all things in the beginning with this goal in mind will consummate his work of *re-creation* on the final day when he brings all things together in unity in his Son, the Lord Jesus (1:10)."[106]

The Savior of the World

Jesus is the Champion who will eliminate the problem of evil. However, giving him lip service alone is insufficient to secure an eternal place with him. The reason is simple. We are part of the problem of evil. The problem arises out of human nature. We want to pursue our desires rather than God's holiness. For example, Paul explained to the Christians at Ephesus that "we all once lived in the passions of our flesh, carrying out the desires of the body and the mind, and were by nature children of wrath, like the rest of mankind" (Ephesians 2:3).

Though we may be delightful people, our natural inclinations put us at odds with God. Because we stand against God, only God can fix our condition. Immediately after Paul describes our nature and passions in Ephesians, he interjects, "But God, being rich in mercy, because of the great love with which he loved us, even when we were dead in our trespasses, made us alive together with Christ—by grace you have been saved..." (Ephesians 2:4-5).

Our personal problem of evil is a microcosmic reflection of the global problem of evil. On both the personal and worldwide level, evil exists because of rebellion against God. The problem is deeper than a cosmetic issue. Only God can do anything about the situation. However, this does not mean that we wait passively for something to happen. To have a right standing individually before God, we must take ownership of Jesus.

To understand how to do this, we look to the book of Romans. Paul writes there, "But the [personal] righteousness based on faith says, 'Do not say in your heart, "Who will ascend into heaven?" (that is, to bring Christ down) or "Who will descend into the abyss?" (that is, to bring Christ up from the dead)" (Romans 10:6-7). In other words, no one is capable of scaling the heights of righteousness or plumbing the depths of injustice. Human understanding cannot satisfy the problem of evil, either on a global or individual level, because we lack a right standing before God. Thankfully, Paul gives us an answer. He goes on to say,

> But what does it [i.e. the righteousness based on faith] say? [Quoting Deuteronomy 30:14], "The word is near you, in your mouth and in your heart" (that is, the word of faith that we [the apostles] proclaim); because, if you confess with your mouth that Jesus is Lord and believe in your heart that God raised him from the dead, you will be saved. For with the heart one believes and is justified, and with the mouth one confesses and is saved.

> —Romans 10:8-10

To confess Jesus as Lord means two things. First, you must recognize him as the risen and returning Champion in the global problem of evil. Second, you must call on him to be your personal Champion to deliver you from your evil. This is the only solution to our personal evil. Your choice will determine whether you enjoy eternal fellowship with Jesus or suffer eternal separation from him. "And there is salvation in no one else, for there is no other name under heaven given among men by which we must be saved" (Acts 4:12).

And so, in the path from grief to eternal life, we have traced the course of God's plan to deal with the problem of evil once for all. God deals with sin judicially by executing justice. He addresses our longings by suffering alongside his people. Because of Jesus' redeeming death on the cross and his resurrection from the dead, we can stand with him. In the resurrection, death will be swallowed up in the victory of eternal life. Our grief follows Jesus' grief full circle. The author of the book of Hebrews writes, "But we see him who for a little while was made lower than the angels, namely Jesus, crowned with glory and honor because of the suffering of death, so that by the grace of God he might taste death for everyone" (Heb. 2:9). He understands our grief completely. All we need to do is trust him for our salvation.

Journal Entry

The Bible accompanies us in our journey from grief and lament to hope and salvation. deliverance from sin is the ultimate cause for praise. The Lord promises to walk with you until he calls them home or returns to judge history. If you belong to him, you can own the promise, "And so we will always be with the Lord" (1 Thessalonians 4:17). Now you know about life and death, grief and hope, and the promise that God offers in his word. If you have yet to trust in Jesus, what is your intention? _____

_____

_____

_____

A Final Note to the Reader

If you have trusted in Jesus to be your Champion, I commend you. You cannot carry on the Christian life by yourself, however. The Bible calls you to join a Bible-believing church and to be baptized as a public testimony of your faith. There, with the help of other believers, you will be able to grow in your faith and to share it with others.

God bless you in your journey.

BIBLIOGRAPHY

Barnhorn, Eleanor. "Why People Prayed for Boston on Twitter and Facebook, and Then Stopped," *Atlantic* online, April 20, 2013. http://www.theatlantic.com/national/archive/2013/04/why-people-prayed-for-boston-on-twitter-and-facebook-and-then-stopped/275137/ (accessed April 21, 2013).

Becker, Amy Julia. "Boundaries in Grief: Why Medicine Should Never Trade Places With a Time to Properly Mourn," *Christianity Today* Online, August 22, 2010. http://www.christianitytoday.com/ct/2010/augustweb-only/43-51.0.html (accessed August 22, 2010).

Blanchard, John, *Where do we Go from Here?* Webster, NY: Evangelical Press, 2008.

Brown, Brenton, and Paul Baloche, "Our God Saves," Colorado Springs: Integrity Music, 2007.

Brueggemann, Walter. *The Prophetic Imagination,* Second Edition. Minneapolis, Fortress Press, 2001.

Dawkins, Richard. *River out of Eden: A Darwinian View of Life.* Basic Books, 1996.

deClaissé-Wolford, Nancy. "Psalm 116: I will Walk in the Land of the Living," Nancy deClaissé-Wolford, Rolf Jacobson, Beth Laneel Tanner, *The Book of Psalms.* Grand Rapids, MI: Eerdmans, 2014.

deSilva, David A. *An Introduction to the New Testament: Contexts, Methods & Ministry Formation.* Downers Grove, IL: IVP Academic, 2004.

Feinberg, Kenneth R. *What is Life Worth? The Unprecedented Effort to Compensate the Victims of 9/11.* New York: Public Affairs, 2005.

Hunter, Cornelius G. *Darwin's God: Evolution and the Problem of Evil.* Grand Rapids, MI: Brazos Press, 2001.

Keller, Timothy. *Walking with God through Pain and Suffering.* New York: Dutton, 2013.

Kübler-Ross, Elisabeth. BusinessBalls.com, "Five Stages of Grief." http:// www.businessballs.com/elisabeth_kubler_ross_five_stages_of_grief. htm (accessed October 6, 2013).

Kushner, Harold S. *When Bad Things Happen to Good People, Twentieth Anniversary Edition.* Knopf Doubleday Publishing Group, 2001, http://books.google.com/books?id=fUd_uhMtai8C&printsec=frontc over&dq=when+bad+things+happen+to+good+people&hl=en&sa= X&ei=W-rjU7qgAo-MyATGp4CwDQ&ved=0CDAQ6AEwAA#v=o nepage&q=when%20bad%20things%20happen%20to%20good%20 people&f=false (accessed August 7, 2014).

Lawrence Paul R. and Nitin Nohria, *Driven: How Human Nature Shapes Our Choices.* San Francisco: Jossey-Bass, 2002.

Legalinsurrection.com, "AG Lynch: Compassion and Love are Best Response to Terror," Wednesday, June 22, 2016. http://legalinsurrection. com/2016/06/ag-lynch-compassion-and-love-are-best-response-to-terror/ (accessed June 24, 2016).

Lange, John Peter. *Psalms*, Commentary on the Holy Scriptures: Critical, Doctrinal and Homiletical. Grand Rapids, MI: Zondervan, 1960.

Lewis, C.S. *The Problem of Pain.* San Fransisco: HarperSanFransisco, 2001.

Mote, Edward. "The Solid Rock" *Hymns of Praise*, 1837.

Moreland, J.P.and Klaus Issler, *The Lost Virtue of Happiness: Discovering the Disciplines of the Good Life*. Colorado Springs: NavPress, 2006.

Mowinckel, Sigmund. *The Psalms in Israel's Worship,* Vol. 1, The Biblical Resource Series, edited by Astrid B. Beck. Grand Rapids, MI: Eerdmans: 2004.

O'Brien, Peter T. *The Letter to the Ephesians,* The Pillar New Testament Commentary, edited by D.A. Carson. Grand Rapids, MI: William B. Eerdmans Publishing Company, 1999.

Piper, John. "In Honor of Tethered Preaching." DesiringGod.org, http://www.desiringgod.org/ResourceLibrary/TasteAndSee/ByDate/2008/3243_In_Honor_of_Tetyhered_Preaching/ (accessed September 18, 2008).

Palumbo, Dennis. *Writing from the Inside Out: Transforming Your Psychological Blocks to Release the Writer Within,* New York: John Wilkey and Sons, Inc., 2000.

Ryken, Leland and Philip Graham Ryken, eds. *The Literary Study Bible.* Wheaton IL: Crossway Bibles, 2007.

Schmutzer, Andrew and Gerald Peterman, *The Theology of Suffering,* Volume One. Chicago: Moody Radio, 2014.

Soulen, Richard N. and R. Kendall Soulen, *Handbook of Biblical Criticism,* Third Edition. Louisville: John Knox Press, 2001.

Stowell, Joseph. *The Trouble with Jesus.* Chicago: Moody Publishers, 2003.

Terrien, Samuel. *The Psalms : Stophic Structure and Theological Commentary.* Grand Rapids: William B. Eerdman's Publishing Company, 2003.

Turner, H.L. "Christ Returneth," http://www.scriptureandmusic.com/Music/Text_Files/Christ_Returneth.html (accessed January 14, 2014).

Walton, J.H. "Garden of Eden." In *Dictionary of the Old Testament Pentateuch,* edited by T. Desmond Alexander and David W. Baker. Downers Grove, IL: InterVarsity Press, 2003.

Walton, John H. and Tremper Longman III. *How to Read Job.* Downers Grove, IL: IVP Academic, 2015.

Westermann, Claus. *Praise and Lament in the Psalms.* Atlanta: John Knox Press, 1981.

Wiker, Benjamin. *Moral Darwinism: How We Became Hedonists.* Downers Grove, IL: InterVarsity Press, 2002.

Wright, H. Norman. *Experiencing Grief,* Nashville: B & H Publishing, 2010.

Wright, N.T. *Surprised by Hope: Rethinking Heaven, the Resurrection, and the Mission of the Church.* New York: Harper Collins, 1989.

Yancey, Philip. *The Bible Jesus Read.* Grand Rapids: Zondervan, 1999.

ENDNOTES

1 H.L. Turner, "Christ Returneth," http://www.scriptureandmusic.com/Music/
   Text_Files/Christ_Returneth.html, accessed January 14, 2014.

2 Joseph Stowell, *The Trouble with Jesus,* (Chicago: Moody Publishers, 2003),
   31-32.

3 Timothy Keller, *Walking with God through Pain and Suffering,* (New York:
   Dutton, 2013), 65.

4 Eleanor Barnhorn, "Why People Prayed for Boston on Twitter and Facebook,
   and Then Stopped," *Atlantic* online, April 20, 2013, accessed from http://www.
   theatlantic.com/national/archive/2013/04/why-people-prayed-for-boston-on-
   twitter-and-facebook-and-then-stopped/275137/, April 21, 2013.

5 Claus Westermann, *Praise and Lament in the Psalms,* (Atlanta: John Knox
   Press, 1981), 160.

6 Harold S. Kushner, *When Bad Things Happen to Good People, Twentieth
   Anniversary Edition*, (Knopf Doubleday Publishing Group, 2001), 51.
   Accessed from http://books.google.com/books?id=fUd_uhMtai8C&printsec
   =frontcover&dq=when+bad+things+happen+to+good+people&hl=en&sa=X
   &ei=W-rjU7qgAo-MyATGp4CwDQ&ved=0CDAQ6AEwAA#v=onepage&
   q=when%20bad%20things%20happen%20to%20good%20people&f=false,
   August 7, 2014.

7 Kushner, *When Bad Things Happen to Good People,* 58-59.

8 All Scripture references are from the English Standard Version (ESV) unless
   otherwise noted.

9 Kushner, *When Bad Things Happen to Good People*, 59.

10 Amy Julia Becker, "Boundaries in Grief: Why Medicine Should Never Trade
   Places With a Time to Properly Mourn," *Christianity Today* Online, August 22,
   2010. Accessed from http://www.christianitytoday.com/ct/2010/augustweb-
   only/43-51.0.html, August 22, 2010.

11 Westermann, *Praise and Lament in the Psalms,* 33.

12 David A. deSilva, *An Introduction to the New Testament: Contexts, Methods
   & Ministry Formation*, (Downers Grove, IL: IVP Academic, 2004), 121.

13 John H. Walton and Tremper Longman III, *How to Read Job,* (Downers Grove,
   IL: IVP Academic, 2015), 59.

14 C.S. Lewis, *The Problem of Pain*, (San Francisco: HarperSanFransisco, 2001), 40.

15 Walton and Longman III, *How to Read Job*, 128.

16 Kushner, *When Bad Things Happen to Good People*, 59.

17 Lewis, *The Problem of Pain*, 91.

18 Kushner, *When Bad Things Happen to Good People*, 51.

19 Kushner, *When Bad Things Happen to Good People*, 58-59.

20 Claus Westermann, *Praise and Lament in the Psalms*, (Atlanta: John Knox Press, 1973), 154. Emphasis added.

21 Walter Brueggemann, *The Prophetic Imagination*, Second Edition, (Minneapolis: Fortress Press, 2001), 93.

22 Claus Westermann, *Praise and Lament in the Psalms*, (Atlanta: John Knox Press, 1973), 170.

23 Westermann, *Praise and Lament in the Psalms*, 28, 29.

24 Westermann, *Praise and Lament in the Psalms*, 34-35.

25 Westermann, *Praise and Lament in the Psalms*, 177.

26 C.S. Lewis, *The Problem of Pain*, (San Francisco: HarperSanFrancisco, 1940, 1996). 155.

27 Aristotle, *Poetics*, (1450b26).

28 Westermann, *Praise and Lament in the Psalms*, 189, 190.

29 Westermann, *Praise and Lament in the Psalms*, 71-72.

30 Westermann, *Praise and Lament in the Psalms*, 79, 80.

31 Westermann, *Praise and Lament in the Psalms*, 105.

32 C.S. Lewis, *The Problem of Pain*,(San Francisco: HarperSanFrancisco, 1940, 1996).

33 C.S. Lewis, *A Grief Observed*, (San Francisco: HarperSanFrancisco, 1961, 1996), 22.

34 Legalinsurrection.com, "AG Lynch: Compassion and Love are Best Response to Terror," Wednesday, June 22, 2016, http://legalinsurrection.com/2016/06/ag-lynch-compassion-and-love-are-best-response-to-terror/ (accessed June 24, 2016).

35 Plato, *Euthyphro*, translated by Lane Cooper, Edith Hamilton and Huntington Cairns, *The Collected Dialogues of Plato, Including the Letters*, (Princeton University, New Jersey: Princeton University Press, 1978), 6d.

36 *Euthyphro*, 4e-5d, paraphrased.

37 *Euthyphro*, 5d, paraphrased.

38 *Euthyphro*, 10a, paraphrased.

39 Together the two psalms form a partial alphabetical acrostic, and the stanza structure is repetitive throughout both. In treating

40 Brueggemann, *The Prophetic Imagination*, 12.

41 John Peter Lange, *Psalms,* Commentary on the Holy Scriptures: Critical, Doctrinal and Homiletical, (Grand Rapids, MI: Zondervan, 1960), 96. Emphasis in the original.

42 R.C. Sproul, Ligonier Ministries Blog, March 10, 2012, "Love God? Sometimes I Hate Him," accessed from http://www.ligonier.org/blog/love-god-sometimes-i-hate-him/, March 26, 2014.

43 Samuel Terrien, *The Psalms: Sophic Structure and Theological Commentary,* (Grand Rapids, MI: Eerdmans, 2003), 554. (Verse numbers adjusted for the English Bible, indentations added for clarity.)

44 *Selah* is a Hebrew poetic notation, possibly calling for the audience to pause and consider what has been said.

45 Using hyphens to signify the Hebrew compound words, the word-for-word translation reads, "But-I-said, 'She to-pierce-me to-change the-right-hand of-the-Most-High.'" Like many languages, Hebrew differentiates nouns by gender. I believe "she" refers to Asaph's grief. My suggested rendering of the verse is, "But I said, 'It is grief that would make me change the right hand of the Most High.'"

46 Hebrew biblical history traces its roots back to the four consecutive Patriarchs, Abraham, Isaac, Jacob, and Joseph. Jewish history begins with Abram, whom God called out of the nations to walk in faith (Genesis 12:1-9). Later God changed the still childless Abram's name to Abraham, "Father of Many Nations" (Genesis 17:1-5). In Abraham's old age, his wife Sarah conceived and gave him Isaac (Genesis 21:1-7). Isaac and his wife Rebekah bore the maternal twin boys Esau and Jacob, with the younger Jacob receiving the family title (Genesis 25:19-28). Jacob is the most colorful character in the four-generation saga, and the Bible gives him considerable coverage (Genesis 25:19-35:29). He is noteworthy for two reasons. First, he sires twelve sons (Genesis 29:1-30:24; 35:16-21), who ultimately become the twelve tribal heads of Israel. Second, Jacob acquires the name "Israel" during an all-night wrestling match with the LORD (Genesis 32:31). Joseph was Jacob's second-to-last son, but ultimately assumed patriarchal rights over his brothers. His story extends from Genesis 37 to the end of the book, chapter 50. The reference in Psalm 77 to 'the children of Jacob and Joseph" (Psalm 77:15) refers to Jacob/Israel's descendants (Exodus 1-2), who became dominant in Egypt because of Joseph's rise to power over the period of his stay there.

47 Sandra L. Burdick and Elizabeth J Turnbull, editors, *God is No Stranger,* (Durham, NC: Light Messages, 2004), 88.

48 Westermann, *Praise and Lament in the Psalms,* 176. Emphasis in original.

49 Westermann, *Praise and Lament in the Psalms,* 184.

50 Westermann, *Praise and Lament in the Psalms,* 155.

51 Westermann, *Praise and Lament in the Psalms,* 159.

52 Westermann, *Praise and Lament in the Psalms,* 159.

53 For centuries well-meaning expositors have placed more blame on Bathsheba than she deserves. Outside of this one place where the text says she was bathing, we see no biblical writer casting blame on Bathsheba. In fact, we can make a case for the opposite in at least one place. When Matthew records Jesus' genealogy, which includes David and Bathsheba's second child, Solomon (see 2 Samuel 2:24-25), Matthew goes through the back door to avoid mentioning her by name. A literal translation of Matthew's account reads, "And David the king begot Solomon through her of Uriah" (Matthew 1:6, author's translation). Matthew mentions three other women by name before this name-avoidance move (Tamar, the mother of the twins, Perez and Zerah in Matthew 1:3; and Rahab the mother of Boaz, along with Ruth the mother of Obed, both in Matthew 1:5). Therefore, he had to have a purpose for avoiding Bathsheba's name. I believe we can find it in Matthew's background. Matthew 9:9-13 records Jesus' call of Matthew, who had been a tax collector for imperial Rome. In that office, he extorted his fellow Jews for personal profit. He may have become rich, but alienated himself. When Jesus uttered his unthinkable call to Matthew to follow him, the call reached out to Matthew as a man. He threw a celebration that involved "tax collectors and sinners" (Matthew 9:11), the most despised people of the day. Matthew knew rejection by reputation firsthand. I am convinced he left Bathsheba's name out of the genealogy to protect her reputation.

54 Kenneth R. Feinberg, transcript from the September 11th Victim Compensation Fund hearings, quoted in *What is Life Worth? The Unprecedented Effort to Compensate the Victims of 9/11,* (New York: Public Affairs, 2005), 139.

55 Philip Yancey, *The Bible Jesus Read,* (Grand Rapids: Zondervan, 1999), 121-122.

56 Yancey, *The Bible Jesus Read,* 121.

57 *Last Action Hero,* 1993.

58 C.S. Lewis, *A Grief Observed,* (San Francisco: HarperSanFrancisco, 1961, 1996), 45.

59 Brueggemann, *The Prophetic Imagination,* Second Edition, ((Minneapolis: Fortress Press, 2001), 46.

60 Westermann, *Praise and Lament in the Psalms,* 119.

61 Brueggemann, *The Prophetic Imagination,* 44.

62 The apostles applied this psalm literally to Judas when they deliberated on a replacement for Judas after his suicide (Acts 1:20).

63 Westermann, *Praise and Lament in the Psalms,* 107.

64 Samuel Terrien, *The Psalms : Stophic Structure and Theological Commentary,* (Grand Rapids: William B. Eerdman's Publishing Company, 2003), 747.

65 Brenton Brown, and Paul Baloche, "Our God Saves," Colorado Springs: Integrity Music, 2007.

66 Edward Mote, "The Solid Rock" *Hymns of Praise,* 1837.

67 Westermann, *Praise and Lament in the Psalms,* 109.

68 In the original language, verse 10 appears to be an affirmation of his personal faith during his crisis. A literal translation is, "I believed [i.e. I had faith] because I spoke—me! / I was greatly afflicted."

69 Westermann, *Praise and Lament in the Psalms,* 159-160.

70 Sigmund Mowinckcel, *The Psalms in Israel's Worship,* Vol. 1, The Biblical Resource Series, ed. Astrid B. Beck, (Grand Rapids, MI: Eerdmans: 2004), 81

71 Nancy Declaisé-Wolford, Rolf A. Jacobson, Beth Laneel Tannor, *The Book of Psalms,* New International Commentary on the Old Testament, Robert L. Hubbard, Jr. ed., (Grand Rapids, MI: Eerdmans Publishing Company, -2014), 861-862. Emphasis in original.

72 Westermann, *Praise and Lament in the Psalms,* 50.

73 Westermann, *Praise and Lament in the Psalms,* 105.

74 Liuan Huska, "Asking Why to Chronic Pain at Age 22," Her.meneutics, January 2013, accessed fromhttp://www.christianitytoday.com/women/2013/january/asking-why-to-chronic-pain-at-age-22.html?utm_source=ctweekly-html&utm_medium=Newsletter&utm_term=8305963&utm_content=149082246&utm_campaign=2013&start=1, January 15, 2013.

75 N.T. Wright, *Surprised by Hope: Rethinking Heaven, the Resurrection, and the Mission of the Church,* (New York: Harper Collins, 1989), 130.

76 Much of Israel's deliverance theology focuses on Jerusalem and the temple. For example, Psalms 53:6; 74:2; and 110:2 all speak of judgment coming out of Zion, the temple mountain in Jerusalem. Amos's prophecy reiterates this sentiment as a warning (Amos 1:2). The prophet Zechariah also sees salvation coming to non-Jews through Zion (Zech. 8:1-3, 22-23). Joel 2:28-3:8, which promises Spirit filling of "all flesh" in the latter days (Joel 2:28), limits the scope of its vision to Jerusalem and Judah (Joel 2:30-3:1).

77 For example, see Matthew 4:12-16; 15:21-28; 28:18-19; Mark 11:15-17; Luke 24:46-47; John 12:20-26.

78 A close examination of Acts chapters 1-17 shows how the early church wrestled with this reality. Jesus stated that the apostles' witness would spread to "Jerusalem and all Judea [Jewish in culture] and Samaria [mixed Jew and Gentile heritage] and to the ends of the earth [the Gentiles]" (Acts 1:8). In the early days of the church, both the apostles and their disciples worshiped in the Jerusalem temple (Acts 2:46) leaving only when they were forced out because of their insistence that Jesus was the promised Messiah of Israel (Acts 4:1-31; 5:1-42). From this point, the believers found themselves at growing odds with Jewish temple worship. The church's break from the temple became complete with Stephen's speech against the temple in Acts 7 and the escalating persecution of the believers in Acts 8. From that point, the followers were forced to abandon a physical temple. Luke, the writer of Acts, placed the second geographical landmark here, when Philip the evangelist took the gospel to the

Samaritan people (Acts 8:4-25). From there, the gospel began to spread to the Gentiles. Following his Samaritan mission, Philip shared the gospel with a high ranking Ethiopian official, opening a gate for the gospel to gain access to Africa (Acts 8:26-40). The gospel to the Gentiles began in earnest when the now converted Saul (who changed his name to the Greek Paul) became an apostle to the Gentiles (Acts 9:1-18). At the same time, Peter witnessed the Spirit's work among God-fearing Gentiles at the house of Cornelius the Roman officer (Acts 10:1-11:18). The event marked a definite thematic change in Acts. The church at Antioch, consisting primarily of Gentile believers, became both the rescuing church for Jerusalem (Acts 11:19-30) and the sending church into the world at large (Acts 13:1-14:28). The magnitude of the shift is evident from Luke's attention to the deep controversy during the Jerusalem Council, when the church elders discussed the requirements of the gospel for Gentiles (Acts 15:1-35).

79 Wright, *Surprised by Hope,* 237.

80 Keller, *Walking with God through Pain and Suffering,* 147.

81 Andrew Schmutzer and Gerald Peterman, *The Theology of Suffering,* Volume One, Lecture Seven, (Chicago: Moody Radio, 2014), Disk 7.

82 Wright, *Surprised by Hope,* 200.

83 Brueggemann, *The Prophetic Imagination,* 56.

84 S.L. McKenzie, "Historiography, Old Testament," *Dictionary of the Old Testament Historical Books: A Compendium of Contemporary Biblical Scholarship,* Bill T. Arnold & H.G.M. Williamson, ed. (Downers Grove, IL: IVP Academic, 2005), 420.

85 Richard N. Soulen and R. Kendall Soulen, *Handbook of Biblical Criticism,* Third Edition, (Louisville: John Knox Press, 2001), "Torah," 198.

86

87 N.T. Wright, *Surprised by Hope,* 75.

88 Wright, *Surprised by Hope,* 282-283.

89 J.P. Moreland and Klaus Issler, *The Lost Virtue of Happiness: Discovering the Disciplines of the Good Life,* (Colorado Springs: NavPress, 2006), 27.

90 Richard Dawkins, *River Out of Eden: A Darwinian View of Life,* (New York: Harper Collins Publishers, 1995), 132-133.

91 Sam Williamson, "Might Modern Worship Be Sort of Like a Cocaine Rush?" Beliefsoftheheart.com, edited from an original posting in June 2012, accessed from http://beliefsoftheheart.com/2013/07/30/might-modern-worship-be-sort-of-like-a-cocaine-rush/#more-2192, March 13, 2015. Emphasis in original.

92 Brueggeman, *The Prophetic Imagination,* 11.

93 C.S. Lewis, *The Lion, the Witch, and the Wardrobe,* (New York: Harper Trophy, 1978), 86.

94 *The Literary Study Bible,* eds. Leland Ryken and Philip Graham Ryken, (Wheaton IL: Crossway Bibles, 2007), 1651.

[95] Likely Epimenides of Crete, *The Literary Study Bible,* 1652.

[96] From Aratus's poem, "Phainomena," *The Literary Study Bible, 1652.*

[97] See Benjamin Wiker, *Moral Darwinism: How We Became Hedonists,* (Downers Grove, IL: InterVarsity Press, 2002), "It All Started with Epicurus," 31-58. "Epicurus counseled his followers to study nature. The reason is rather strange. The goal of the study of nature was not, as one might think, the discovery of the truth. The goal, oddly enough, was to produce and maintain a certain condition of mind, a state of being undisturbed or untroubled," 32.

[98] See Keller, *Walking with God through Pain and Suffering,* 37-39.

[99] John Blanchard, *Where do we Go from Here?* (Webster, NY: Evangelical Press, 2008), 21.

[100] O'Brien, *Ephesians,* 111-112. Emphasis in original.

[101] Even theistic evolution, the idea that God used evolutionary processes, tries to rob God of his creative power.

[102] Paul R. Lawrence and Nitin Nohria, *Driven: How Human Nature Shapes Our Choices,* (San Francisco: Jossey-Bass, 2002), 21-22.

[103] Cornelius G. Hunter, *Darwin's God: Evolution and the Problem of Evil,* (Grand Rapids, MI: Brazos Press, 2001), 16.

[104] For example, see Luke 13:1-5, where Jesus addresses a question regarding Herod's terrorist act against a group of Galilean worshipers. In his reply, he mentions an incident where a tower in Siloam collapsed and killed eighteen people. He leaves their question unanswered and takes the dialogue in another direction for two reasons. One, they had the Old Testament resources to answer the theodicy question. Two, they had ignored the larger issue, "What will you do with Jesus?" The question about Jesus drives the entire section on Jesus' journey to Jerusalem, from Luke 9:51-19:40.

[105] J.H. Walton, "Garden of Eden," in *Dictionary of the Old Testament Pentateuch,* eds. T. Desmond Alexander and David W. Baker (Downers Grove, IL: InterVarsity Press, 2003), 205.

[106] O'Brien, *The Letter to the Ephesians,* 244. Emphasis in original.

Printed in the United States
By Bookmasters